CONFERENCE PROCEEDINGS

T0306639

Afghanistan: State and Society, Great Power Politics, and the Way Ahead

Findings from an International Conference, Copenhagen, Denmark, 2007

Editors

Cheryl Benard, Ole Kværnø, Peter Dahl Thruelsen, Kristen Cordell

Contributors

Peter Viggo Jakobsen, Michael Rubin, Mikkel Vedby Rasmussen, Ali Alfoneh, Angel Rabasa, Pavel K. Baev, Cheryl Benard, Samina Ahmed, Ali Jalali, Peter Dahl Thruelsen, Obaid Younossi, Khalid Nadiri

RAND CENTER FOR MIDDLE EAST PUBLIC POLICY

International Programs at RAND

This research was conducted within the Initiative for Middle Eastern Youth and the RAND Center for Middle East Public Policy. The Initiative for Middle Eastern Youth is funded by donations from private individuals and sources in the State of Qatar. The RAND Center for Middle East Public Policy, part of International Programs at the RAND Corporation, aims to improve public policy by providing decisionmakers and the public with rigorous, objective research on critical policy issues affecting the Middle East.

Library of Congress Cataloging-in-Publication Data

Afghanistan : state and society, great power politics, and the way ahead : findings from an international conference, Copenhagen, Denmark, 2007 / Cheryl Benard ... [et al.].
p. cm.
Includes bibliographical references.
ISBN 978-0-8330-4415-0 (pbk. : alk. paper)
1. Afghanistan—Politics and government—2001——Congresses. 2. Afghanistan—Foreign relations—Congresses. 3. Nation-building—Afghanistan—Congresses. I. Benard, Cheryl, 1953–

DS371.4.A3844 2008
958.104'7—dc22

2008014940

The RAND Corporation is a nonprofit research organization providing objective analysis and effective solutions that address the challenges facing the public and private sectors around the world. RAND's publications do not necessarily reflect the opinions of its research clients and sponsors.

Published 2008 by the RAND Corporation
1776 Main Street, P.O. Box 2138, Santa Monica, CA 90407-2138
1200 South Hayes Street, Arlington, VA 22202-5050
4570 Fifth Avenue, Suite 600, Pittsburgh, PA 15213-2665
RAND URL: http://www.rand.org/
To order RAND documents or to obtain additional information, contact
Distribution Services: Telephone: (310) 451-7002;
Fax: (310) 451-6915; Email: order@rand.org

Preface

This volume compiles a selection of papers presented at a June 2007 conference titled "Afghanistan: State and Society, Great Power Politics, and the Way Ahead." The conference was held in Copenhagen and hosted by the Royal Danish Defence College, the RAND Initiative for Middle Eastern Youth, and the RAND Center for Middle East Public Policy.

This product is part of the RAND Corporation's Conference Proceedings series. RAND conference proceedings present a collection of papers delivered at a conference or a summary of the conference. The material herein has been vetted by the conference attendees, and both the introduction and the post-conference material have been reviewed and approved for publication by the RAND Center for Middle East Public Policy.

The RAND Initiative for Middle Eastern Youth is funded by donations from private individuals and sources in the State of Qatar. The RAND Center for Middle East Public Policy (CMEPP), part of International Programs at RAND, aims to improve public policy by providing decisionmakers and the public with rigorous, objective research on critical policy issues affecting the Middle East.

For more information on the RAND Center for Middle East Public Policy, contact the Director, David Aaron. He can be reached by email at David_Aaron@rand.org; by phone at 310-393-0411, extension 7782; or by mail at RAND, 1776 Main Street, Santa Monica, California 90407-2138.

For more information on the Initiative for Middle Eastern Youth, contact the Director, Cheryl Benard. She can be reached via email at Cheryl_Benard@rand.org; by phone at 703-413-110, extension 5379; or by mail at RAND, 1200 South Hayes Street, Arlington, Virginia 22202-5050.

Contents

Figures and Tables

Figures

Tables

Acknowledgments

The RAND Corporation would like to thank their partners at the Royal Danish Defence College for their gracious sponsorship of this event. Jointly, we thank those who participated in the event and shared their papers for publication.

Abbreviations

AMF	Afghan Military Forces
ANA	Afghan National Army
ANAP	Afghan National Auxiliary Police
ANP	Afghan National Police
DDR	Disarmament Demobilization and Reintegration
DIAG	Disarmament of Illegal Armed Groups
FATA	Federally Administered Tribal Areas
GDP	gross domestic product
ISAF	International Security Assistance Force
NATO	North Atlantic Treaty Organization
NWA	North Waziristan Agency
NWFP	North West Frontier Provence
SWA	South Waziristan Agency
USAID	United States Agency for International Development

CHAPTER 1

Introduction

Peter Dahl Thruelsen and Kristen Cordell[1]

Five years after the U.S.-led coalition initiated its attack on al Qaeda training camps and the Taliban government in Afghanistan, peace is yet to be won. The rapid collapse of the Taliban regime created a security vacuum in vast parts of the country that was soon filled by local warlords and mid-level commanders. The lack of international military presence in the periphery, especially in the South, provided a safe haven for the retreating Taliban to rebuild and expand their power base.

In May of 2007, the International Security Assistance Force, led by NATO, took over coordination of international activities in Afghanistan. Transitional power sharing and coordination, along with the tactical, logistical, and managerial necessities of the mission, introduced novel challenges. In addition to these organizational shifts, International Security Assistance Force (ISAF) forces have been continually challenged by the Taliban-led insurgency in southern and eastern Afghanistan, illicit opium production, undeveloped security structures, lack of political control in the provinces, and large-scale corruption within governmental institutions.

Nation building, a core goal of the ISAF mission, has focused on overcoming these challenges through development of a viable state infrastructure. Reforms in the areas of security, governance, justice, and economic stability have been advanced through partnerships between ISAF and local actors on the ground. An example of nation-building success can be seen in the presidential, parliamentary, and district elections, which have been held in a country characterized by decades of political instability. Advances in gender equity can be seen across sectors, as girls enjoy growing access to education and women take their place in governmental institutions and democratic processes as voters, elected officials, and administrators. The nation-building effort has made many achievements, but it also faces a host of old and new challenges.

It was against this backdrop of advancement and transition that in June 2007, the RAND Corporation along with the Royal Danish Defence College hosted an international conference entitled "Afghanistan: State and Society, Great Power Politics, and the Way Ahead." This two-day event, held in Copenhagen, was attended by more than 100 politicians, scholars, academics, officers, and representative of both governmental and nongovernmental institutions from more than 20 different states. The aim of the event was to address problems and obstacles and to suggest solutions. Papers were presented by practitioners, policymakers, and academics on a

[1] Peter Dahl Thruelsen is a research fellow at the Institute for Strategy at the Royal Danish Defence College. His main areas of research are conflict resolution, nation building, security sector reform, and peacekeeping/enforcement. Kristen Cordell is a research assistant at the RAND Corporation, where she specializes in youth and gender issues in the Middle East.

wide variety of topics relating to the Afghan state. Themes that emerged included the importance of historical precedents, the role of coordination among relevant parties, and the development of an all-encompassing, long-term strategic approach.

CHAPTER TWO

U.S. Interests and Stakes in Afghanistan: In for the Long Haul or Gone Tomorrow?

Peter Viggo Jakobsen[1]

After the September 11 attacks, the United States went to war in Afghanistan and subsequently Iraq, arguing that national and vital interests were at stake. U.S. words and actions signaled strong resolve and a commitment to stay engaged until the American objectives had been met. Now things look very different. Neither operation has gone according to plan. In Iraq, the United States is headed for the exit without having achieved its initial objectives, and in Afghanistan, a resurgent Taliban is testing the United States' and NATO's commitment to nation-building. This raises the question whether the United States will stay engaged in Afghanistan or be forced to a premature Iraqi-style departure.

To address this question, this paper first identifies the interests that states are willing to use force to promote and protect. These interests serve as an analytical tool for assessing the strength of the U.S. commitment and willingness to stay the course in Afghanistan. This indicator cannot stand alone, however. The interests that motivate a state to go to war may change once the battle has been joined. Defeats and setbacks on the battlefield may cause a state to reassess its interests. Interests that looked "vital" at the start of the conflict may not look so vital after all when the costs and casualties pile up and victory remains elusive. The Vietnam War is a case in point. In its initial phases, the war was perceived as vital to preventing Communist expansion. After the war was lost, the U.S. involvement came to be seen as a costly mistake in a peripheral part of the world. Since the interests invoked at the start of a war are poor predictors of a state's willingness to stay engaged if things go wrong, four indicators will be used to assess the American willingness to stay in Afghanistan for the long haul: casualties, political leadership, elite consensus, and purpose of the operation/prospects for success.

Interests and the Use of Force

States generally invoke four different types of interests to justify their use of force: vital interest, strategic interest, stability interest, and moral/ideological interest.[2] *Vital interest* refers to the defense of the homeland. The willingness to threaten and use force and suffer pain is assumed to be highest when an act of aggression threatens the homeland directly. *Strategic interest* refers

[1] Peter Viggo Jakobsen is an associate professor for the Department of Political Science at the University of Copenhagen.

[2] Peter Viggo Jakobsen, *Western Use of Coercive Diplomacy After the Cold War: A Challenge for Theory and Practice*, New York: Macmillan Press, 1998, pp. 35–38.

to the preservation of an acceptable balance of power, be it global or regional. The interest here is to prevent areas outside the homeland of great economic and strategic importance from falling into the wrong hands or descending into chaos. Protection of access to important raw materials and important trade links fall into this category, and the American involvement in Europe during both World Wars was motivated by this interest.

Stability interest is related to the preservation of stability in countries close to home. This interest may induce governments to threaten and use force to stop conflicts that do not threaten the regional balance of power and pose little threat to national security and economic prosperity. Governments may see an interest in taking action vis-à-vis conflicts that they would have ignored had they been further from home, in order to reduce their destabilizing effects, such as economic breakdown, refugee flows, agitation, and terrorism among expatriate groups and the spread of the conflict to hitherto peaceful neighboring countries.

Moral/ideological interest is related to the protection of values and ideas concerning world order, principles of international law, systems of government, and human rights.

All the interests listed here are important in the sense that they may induce governments to threaten and use force. Their ranking suggests that economic and military interests are more important than ideological and moral ones, and that governments are least likely to threaten and use force and suffer pain when the latter interests are at stake, and most likely to do so when they are facing a direct threat to their economic and military security. If more than one type of interest is involved in the same conflict, the willingness to threaten and use force is expected to increase.

Short- Versus Long-Term Commitments

Once the battle has been joined, the perceived interest and willingness to stay the course is affected by events on the ground. Unexpected setbacks or a high level of casualties may induce states to reassess their commitment and withdraw before their objectives have been met. Casualties are often seen as the single most important factor affecting the willingness of a state to stay the course. While casualties are indeed a factor, they are by no means the most important one. The *interpretation* of casualties—whether the soldiers are dying in vain—matters more than the number per se. Three factors determine how a rise in casualties affects the willingness and ability of a state to sustain a long-term commitment.[3]

1. Political Leadership. It is important that the government has made its case for war, prepared the public for casualties, and explained why the stakes involved warrant high costs in terms of blood and treasure. If political and public support is not high when casualties are taken, then mobilizing such support will be an uphill struggle. Proactive leadership with respect to justifying the use of force and its likely costs is therefore necessary in order to mobilize and sustain political and popular support for a military engagement.

2. Degree of Political/Elite Consensus. In the U.S. context, a bipartisan consensus is necessary to sustain a costly long-term military commitment. If the President can mobilize and sustain political support for a military operation and avoid a situation in which rising costs and casualties trigger calls for withdrawal from the Hill and the media, then an operation is likely

---

[3] The framework is laid out in greater detail in my "Har Danmark et body bag syndrom?" [Does Denmark Have a Body Bag Syndrome?], *Militært Tidsskrift*, Vol. 133, No. 1, April 2004, pp. 94–114.

to continue to enjoy popular support, as the public usually takes their cue from the opinion leaders that they trust.

3. Purpose of the Operation/Prospects for Success. Finally, it is important that the cause is considered just and worthwhile and that victory is expected. A belief in victory is absolutely crucial in order to sustain a long-term commitment if the costs are considerable. If victory appears unattainable, elites and the public will lose heart and begin to pressure the government to withdraw, as was the case in Vietnam and currently is in Iraq.

Perceived U.S. Interests in Afghanistan After 9/11

An analysis of statements made by members of the Bush Administration after 9/11 shows that three of the four types of interests outlined above are perceived to be at stake:

- *Vital:* Prevent another 9/11 Al Qaeda attack.
- *Strategic*: Prevent regions (Afghanistan and Pakistan) from falling in the hands of the Taliban and Islamist terrorists; Afghanistan is portrayed as a major front in the global/long war on terror.
- *Moral/ideological:* Build democracy, enhance human and especially women's rights; part of a new ideological struggle against Islamist militants.

Against this background, the initial decision to go to war and the subsequent decisions to enhance the U.S. commitment as the operation ran into trouble were overdetermined. With so many interests perceived to be at stake, this was to be expected, and it also leads one to predict a long-term U.S. commitment to Afghanistan.

U.S. Interests Versus Commitments to Date

This prediction is qualified by the existing gap between American words and deeds. President Bush's call for a new Marshall Plan for Afghanistan[4] and the many references to vital U.S. interests made by government representatives have not been backed up by the military and economic commitments that such rhetoric implies. The initial Afghanistan strategy aimed at winning a quick and decisive victory with a minimum involvement of U.S. forces on the ground. Once this had been achieved, the Bush Administration sought to give the UN and its friends and allies the principal responsibility for nation-building. Fear of a Soviet-style quagmire, an ideological distaste for nation-building, and pressing business in Iraq resulted in a "nation-building lite" approach that sought to achieve U.S. objectives in Afghanistan on the cheap.[5] As a result, the Bush Administration has consistently been criticized by analysts and the Democrats in Congress for doing too little too late in Afghanistan.

At the same time, it is important to stress that the Bush Administration has given far greater priority to Afghanistan than anyone else. The United States is by far the no. 1 contribu-

---

[4] White House Office of the Press Secretary, "President Outlines War Effort," April 17, 2002.

[5] Michael Ignatieff, "Nation-Building Lite," *New York Times Magazine*, July 28, 2002, Section 6, p. 26; Peter Viggo Jakobsen, *PRTs in Afghanistan: Successful But Not Sufficient*, Danish Institute for International Studies, DIIS Report 2005: 6, p. 8.

tor of troops (25.000 compared with a NATO total of some 35.500; the no. 2 contributor is the United Kingdom with 7.700);[6] it has suffered the majority of the casualties (337 compared with a coalition total of 538);[7] it has provided most of the military assistance to Afghan security forces ($6 billion); and, finally, it also leads the field with respect to reconstruction and development aid ($4.4 billion).[8] The United States accounts for some 50 percent of reconstruction funding and has spent four times as much as the next-highest donor, Japan.[9] A total of $99 billion has been committed by the United States in the 2001–2007 period.[10]

More important in terms of future staying power, the United States has reacted to the mounting problems and the return of the Taliban by increasing its commitments. This happened for the first time following a policy review in 2003 and again in February 2007, when the Bush Administration presented a $12.3 billion budget request to support the Afghan security forces and reconstruction and development.[11] The United States has also played a key role in pressuring the international community, and in particular NATO governments, to do more. The United States has put NATO's future on the line, making it clear to the other members that failure is not an option.[12]

Is the U.S. Commitment Sustainable?

Judging from the indicators introduced above, the U.S. commitment does look sustainable for the near-medium term. The number of U.S. casualties to date is not alarming. Although the 337 deaths are high by contemporary standards, they are nevertheless small when compared with the more than 3.500 U.S. soldiers killed in Iraq as of June 2007. Key to the future is therefore how the other three indicators develop.

1. Political Leadership. The Bush Administration has shown leadership throughout the conflict, most recently in its efforts to promote its new six-point plan for Afghanistan strategy and in its efforts to pressure NATO to do more.[13] Yet, Presidential leadership has been reluctant and reactive. President Bush has primarily reacted to pressure from critics and crises.

---

6 JoAnne O'Bryant and Michael Waterhouse, *U.S. Forces in Afghanistan*, CRS Report for Congress, RS22633, March 27, 2007, p. 1; NATO, ISAF fact sheet, no date; OK Ministry of Defence, Operations in Afghanistan: British forces.

7 "Coalition Casualties in Afghanistan," Wikipedia, accessed on June 16, 2007: http://en.wikipedia.org/wiki/Coalition_casualties_in_Afghanistan.

8 U.S. Government Accountability Office, *Securing, Stabilizing, and Reconstructing Afghanistan: Key Issues for Congressional Oversight*, GAO-07-801SP, May 2007, pp. 13, 28.

9 Seema Patel and Steven Ross, *Breaking Point: Measuring Progress in Afghanistan*, Washington, D.C.: Center for Strategic and International Studies, 2007, p. 68; Senlis Council, "Afghanistan Five Years Later: The Return of the Taliban," Spring/Summer 2006, Chapter 5, p. 21.

10 Amy Belasco, *The Cost of Iraq, Afghanistan, and Other Global War on Terror Operations Since 9/11*, CRS Report for Congress, RL33110, March 14, 2007, p. 8.

11 U.S. Government Accountability Office, *Securing, Stabilizing, and Reconstructing Afghanistan: Key Issues for Congressional Oversight*, GAO-07-801SP, May 2007, p. 1.

12 Barnett R. Rubin, "Still Ours to Lose: Afghanistan on the Brink," prepared testimony for the House Committee on International Relations, September 20, 2006, and the Senate Committee on Foreign Relations, September 21, 2006.

13 U.S. Department of State, "Bush Announces New Plan for Afghanistan," February 15, 2007.

2. Degree of Political/Elite Consensus. The Afghanistan operation continues to enjoy a strong bipartisan consensus as well as support from the media. There is almost universal agreement that Afghanistan must not again become a haven for terrorists,[14] and the Administration has time and again come under fire for doing too little about the "forgotten" war in Afghanistan.[15]

3. Purpose of the Operation/Prospects for Success. The purpose is hard to disagree with: Prevent new terrorist attacks on the United States and help to improve living standards and build democracy. The prospects for success are the weak link in the chain. The news stories from Afghanistan are mainly negative, and so are the reports and articles published by international think tanks and regional experts. While most still agree that Afghanistan, unlike Iraq, remains "winnable," there is also widespread agreement that Afghanistan may be lost unless radical improvements are made relatively quickly.[16] The big question that ultimately will determine U.S. staying power is therefore whether the U.S. government can continue to convince the Afghans, the international community, and its own citizens that victory is achievable.

Is the U.S. Commitment Enough?

In light of the problems that the Afghanistan operation is currently facing, the recent increases in the U.S. commitment may not be enough. The operation remains seriously undermanned and underfunded in comparison to other recent nation-building operations. The $57 per capita provided in external economic aid during the first two years of the Afghanistan operation is much lower than the $679 in Bosnia, $233 in East Timor, $526 in Kosovo, and $206 in Iraq. Similarly, there are 2 international soldiers per 1.000 inhabitants in Afghanistan versus a peak deployment of 17 in Bosnia, 10 in East Timor, 20 in Kosovo, and 7 in Iraq (2003).[17] As is clear from Table 1, Afghanistan does not meet any of RAND's criteria for nation-building success, and the Afghan National Army's 42.000 personnel, which is projected to increase to 70.000 in 2008, do little to fill the gap in the security field.[18]

Since the number of international troops and police is unlikely to increase significantly, the only way to address the security gap is to increase the size of the Afghan forces. In this light, the recent decision to create a temporary 20.000-strong Afghan National Auxiliary Police makes a lot of sense.[19]

---

14 This is also one of the conclusions in the *9/11 Commission Report: Final Report of the National Commission on Terrorist Attacks Upon the United States* (New York: W. W. Norton, 2004, pp. 369–371).

15 See for instance, "Afghanistan: The Other War," *Time*, March 8, 2004; "Afghanistan's Forgotten War," *New York Times*, August 6, 2005; Charles M. Sennott, "Afghanistan: After 5 Years, a Forgotten War?" *Boston Globe*, September 12, 2006. Interestingly, the U.S. media has also been criticized for ignoring Afghanistan: Sherry Ricchiardi, "The Forgotten War," *American Journalism Review*, August–September 2006.

16 See for instance Michael Fumento, "The Other War: Afghanistan Is Winnable, but Victory Can't Be Taken for Granted," *The Weekly Standard*, Vol. 12, No. 37, June 11, 2007.

17 James Dobbins et al., *The UN's Role in Nation-Building: From the Congo to Iraq*, Santa Monica, Calif.: RAND Corporation, MG-304-RC, 2005, pp. 228, 239.

18 Afghanistan National Development Strategy, "Benchmark Status Report March 2006 to March 2007," April 2007, p. 3.

19 "Afghanistan: Gov't Bid to Boost Police in South," *IRIN News*, March 4, 2007.

Table 2.1
RAND Criteria for Success Applied to Afghanistan

RAND Success Criteria	Requirements	Current Commitment/Capacity	Shortfalls
100 international military per 10.000 inhabitants	285.000	60.500	224.500
15 international police per 10.000 inhabitants	42.750	Some 650 police advisors and mentors[a]	42.100
20 domestic police per 10.000 inhabitants	57.000	63.000+ trained but only 30.395 were considered "trained and equipped to carry out their police functions" in June 2006[b]	26.605
$250 per capita in external economic assistance during first two years	$250 per capita	$57 per capita	$193 per capita

SOURCE: Seth G. Jones et al., *Establishing Law and Order After Conflict*, Santa Monica, Calif.: RAND Corporation, MG-374-RC, 2005, p. xiii.

NOTE: Based on UN Development Programme population estimate of 28.500.000.

[a] This figure is made up of American, German, and EU contributions. It includes 195 personnel from the EUPOL Afghanistan force, which is not yet fully deployed. See German Federal Foreign Office, German Federal Ministry of the Interior, "Afghanistan for Rebuilding the Police Force in Afghanistan," May 29, 2006, and DynCorp International, "IG Report Praises DI Police Training in Afghanistan," press release, December 4, 2006.

[b] Interagency Assessment of Afghanistan Police Training and Readiness, Inspectors General, U.S. Dept. of State and U.S. Dept. of Defense, November 2006, p. 15.

With respect to economic assistance, the three international donor conferences held to date in Tokyo (2002), Berlin (2004), and London (2006) have resulted in pledges totalling $23.9 billion. Most of this aid has failed to materialize, however. Of the $13.4 billion pledged at the first two conferences, only $3.3 billion had been implemented in reconstruction projects by February 2005.[20] Experts estimate that the international community must double its economic assistance to Afghanistan and that some $3 billion a year will be required.[21]

More resources are not sufficient for success, however. Policy changes virtually across the board are also required. There is a widespread agreement among independent experts that the following problems, at a minimum, need to be addressed in order to prevent the situation from deteriorating further:[22]

- lack of overall coordination of the international efforts
- a failed and counterproductive narcotics policy
- Pakistani sanctuary and support for the Taliban
- corruption at all levels of government
- a nonfunctioning judicial sector
- overreliance on airpower, creating too many civilian casualties.

---

20 Carl Robichaud, "Remember Afghanistan? A Glass Half Full, On the Titanic," *World Policy Journal*, Vol. 23, No. 1, Spring 2006, p. 21.

21 Robichaud, "Remember Afghanistan?" p. 21; Barry R. Rubin, "Saving Afghanistan," *Foreign Affairs*, Vol. 86, No. 1, January–February 2007.

22 Associated Press, "Afghan Civilians Reportedly Killed More by U.S., NATO Than Insurgents," *U.S. Today*, June 24, 2007; Karl F. Inderfurth, "Losing the 'Other War' in Afghanistan?" *International Herald Tribune*, May 29, 2007; Seema Patel and Steven Ross, *Breaking Point: Measuring Progress in Afghanistan*, Washington, D.C.: Center for Strategic and International Studies, 2007; Peter van Ham and Jorrit Kamminga, "Poppies for Peace: Reforming Afghanistan's Opium Industry," *Washington Quarterly*, Vol. 30, No. 1, Winter 2006–2007, pp. 69–81.

Meeting all these challenges will be extremely difficult, and it remains an open question whether the international community will be capable of doing this before Western publics lose confidence in the coalition's ability to win. If this confidence is lost, Western governments will be forced to withdraw or scale down their involvement in Afghanistan, just like the coalition in Iraq.

Conclusion

This paper has argued that the United States perceives vital, strategic, and moral/ideological interests to be at stake in Afghanistan and that this should translate into a long-term commitment and willingness to suffer considerable casualties and other costs. This prediction is qualified somewhat by the fact that the United States has tried to achieve its objectives in Afghanistan on the cheap. The gap between words and deeds has been and remains considerable.

This said, the United States is by far the single most important contributor of troops and funds to Afghanistan. More important, the United States has so far reacted to setbacks by increasing its commitments, and the United States has also been instrumental in pressuring the international community, and especially NATO, to do more.

Four factors will determine the length and strength of the U.S. commitment to Afghanistan: casualties, political leadership, elite consensus, and the purpose of the operation/prospects for success. Casualties are not likely to become a major issue in the near term because the casualties suffered in Afghanistan are ten times smaller than the casualties suffered by U.S. forces in Iraq. The Bush Administration has demonstrated the political leadership necessary at home and abroad to mobilize and sustain support for the engagement in Afghanistan and continues to do so. There is strong bipartisan and media support for a continued U.S. commitment. Failure in Afghanistan is perceived as likely to increase the risk of another 9/11, and the sentiment that Afghanistan cannot be allowed to fall is likely to be strengthened by the U.S. failure in Iraq. U.S. policymakers can be expected to go to great lengths to avoid a situation where the United States is seen to have lost two wars in a row.

Ultimately, the length of the U.S. commitment will be determined by events on the ground, however. It is therefore critical to improve the prospects for success. The number of reports questioning whether Afghanistan is winnable and whether the United States and NATO can stay the course has grown in recent months. The only way to silence the skeptics is to invest more resources in Afghanistan and to show visible progress on the ground. Whether this is possible remains an open question. What remains certain is that continued U.S. leadership will be necessary to turn the situation around. Success is only possible if the United States increases its commitment and continues its diplomatic efforts to convince and cajole the Afghan government, Pakistan, and the international community at large to do more to support the efforts to stabilize the country. U.S. leadership has been critical in mobilizing and sustaining support for Afghanistan to date, and it will be the sine qua non in order to sustain a long-term international commitment as well.

CHAPTER 3

Understanding Iranian Strategy in Afghanistan

Michael Rubin[1]

While stories of Iranian malfeasance in Iraq concern U.S. policymakers and are subject to U.S. domestic media coverage, Afghanistan is as important to Iranian policymakers as it is to their U.S. and NATO counterparts. While an Iraq free of Iranian influence would pose a challenge to the religious legitimacy of the Iranian leadership, Iranians have reconciled themselves to the fact that Iraq is distinct from Iran and that the border, however disputed along its margins, is a legitimate division between two entities. Many Iranians feel, however, that Tehran has a legitimate historical claim to Afghanistan. Regardless of religiosity, Iranian nationalists see Afghanistan as part of Iran's near-abroad. Their sentiment toward their Afghan neighbors parallels the attitude of Russian nationalists who believe that they should have predominant influence among the territories of the former Soviet Union. From an Iranian perspective, Afghan independence is the result only of British interference and an accident of history. This belief underlies Iranian strategy in Afghanistan.

Historical Background

To understand current Iranian strategy in Afghanistan, it is essential to understand Iranian claims to influence. Iranian interest in Afghanistan dates back millennia. What is now Afghanistan was part of the ancient Persian Achaemenid Empire. While the Arab invasion of Iran ended Persian predominance on the Iranian plateau, the Persian Samanid dynasty (819–899) reincorporated Afghanistan as a Persian-ruled domain in the ninth century. The fifteenth-century Qara Qoyunlu dynasty leader Jahan Shah (r. 1438–1467) briefly established Herat as the capital of his Iranian domains, albeit briefly. In the early sixteenth century, the Safavid Shah Tahmasp (r. 1524–1576) drove the Uzbeks from Herat for a short time but, by century's end, Shah Abbas (r. 1587–1629) had re-asserted Iranian dominance over the city and all of western Afghanistan. Dominance went both ways. As Safavid power waned in the early eighteenth century, an Afghan commander operating from Herat conquered much of Iran, declared himself Shah, and again established the Afghan city as the capital of domains spread across both countries, although, again, squabbling among his sons and successors led to the city's loss.

In the early nineteenth century, the Qajar dynasty ruler Muhammad Shah (r. 1834–1848) sought to reassert Iran's claim to Herat. He marched on the city in 1837, but the international

[1] Michael Rubin is a resident scholar at the American Enterprise Institute for Public Policy Research, a senior lecturer at the Naval Postgraduate School's Center for Civil Military Relations, and editor of the *Middle East Quarterly*.

milieu had changed. British policymakers, believing India to be vulnerable to an overland invasion from Russia, were no longer indifferent to Afghan affairs. They worried that the Iranian Shah might offer the Tsar's army transit and so resolved to keep Afghanistan under informal British influence. British pressure forced Muhammad Shah to withdraw his army.

From an Iranian perspective, though, the Afghan issue had less to do with Great Game strategy and more to do with prestige and national security. Most residents of Herat did—and still do—speak Persian. Muhammad Shah had backed down, but both he and his successor, Nasir al-Din Shah (r. 1848–1896), did not accept that Iran's claim to Herat had lapsed. While the British looked at Herat as the key to India, the Shah viewed the city as the key to Khurasan, Iran's breadbasket. Without possession of the city and the natural boundaries of its mountains, it became more difficult for Iranian troops to defend the shrine city of Mashhad and nearby towns from marauding Turkmen tribesmen whom, the Iranian ambassador in Paris claimed, had enslaved more than 150,000 Iranians.[2]

The new shah took action. In October 1856, Iranian troops seized Herat. What came next was unprecedented and caught the Iranian government by surprise. Iranian wars had always been fought on land. A couple weeks after Iranian troops raised the Shah's pennant in Herat, British authorities in Bombay dispatched 45 ships carrying almost 6,000 troops. They seized the Iranian port of Bushehr and pushed inland. The Shah sued for peace. In the 1857 Treaty of Paris, the Shah relinquished all claim to Afghanistan, and, in return, the British forces withdrew. One of the greatest "what-ifs" of Iranian history involves the timing of the march on Herat: A few months after hostilities ceased, India erupted into full-scale revolt. The British garrison in India had no forces to spare as they struggled to put down the Mutiny, going so far as to ship cannons seized in Iran back to India for use in battle against the Sepoy rebels. Iranian officials at the time quipped that had Iranian forces invaded Herat only a few months later, the British forces would have been too bogged down to respond.[3] Furthering the humiliation, it was British military engineers who demarcated the border two decades later, when a new dispute arose.[4] Resentment and a sense of being shortchanged by history pervades Iranian education to this day. Elementary school geography textbooks continue to list Herat (as well as Dagestan, similarly lost in war to a foreign power) as provinces of Iran.

While successive Iranian governments reconciled themselves to the loss of Afghanistan—they have not re-asserted a sovereign claim as some figures in the Islamic Republic have with Bahrain[5]—Iranian leaders have not remained aloof from Afghan affairs. Throughout much of the twentieth century, common conservative interests muted disputes. Both monarchies faced common enemies and threats from the same social movements. In 1921, they concluded a Treaty of Friendship, and, in 1934, they resolved through arbitration—in Afghanistan's favor—a border dispute. Three years later, both monarchies, along with Turkey and Iraq, signed the Saadabad Pact, in which they agreed to respect each other's territorial integrity and

---

[2] Farrukh Khan, "Respecting Wishes of the Persian Government," Paris, December 26, 1857. FO 60/221.

[3] 'Abd Allah Mustawfi, *Shahr-i zindigani-i man ya tarikh-i ijtima'i va idari-i dawrah-'i qajariyah* [The Town of My Life or the History of Society and Administration of the Qajar Era], Tehran: Kitabfurushi-i Zavvar, 1964, pp. 85–86 .

[4] Sir Frederic John Goldsmid and Sir Oliver St. John, *Eastern Persia: An Account of the Journeys of the Persian Boundary Commission, 1870–71–72*, London: Macmillan and Co., 1876.

[5] Husayn Shariatmadari, *Ahvaz-i Kucheh-i Baghi* [Street Garden Song], Kayhan (Tehran), July 9, 2007, p. 2.

refrain from aggression against each other, and, two years later, they resolved amicably a water-sharing dispute.

Tensions increased markedly with the 1979 Islamic Revolution. Ayatollah Ruhollah Khomeini criticized the Afghan government even prior to his return to Tehran. He amplified his vitriol as the Soviet-sponsored government consolidated control.[6] Iran was a full player by proxy in the Afghan civil war, assisting a loose coalition of Persian, Shi'a, and Turkic factions against the Pakistan and Saudi-supported Pushtuns. Tensions between Iran and Afghanistan climaxed with the Taliban takeover and consolidation of much of the country. In 1998, after the Taliban massacred nine Iranian diplomats and intelligence officials, the two countries almost went to war. Nevertheless, Tehran and Kabul maintained discreet ties. The 9/11 Commission found that the Iranian authorities granted free passage to al Qaeda operatives training in Taliban-controlled territory, including between eight and ten of the 9/11 hijackers.[7]

Iranian Strategy

For Iran, influence in Afghanistan appears to be a zero-sum game. While the Iranian government welcomed the Taliban's fall, they were less than sanguine about the actions of Washington to precipitate it. While Iranian and American diplomats cooperated to form a post-Taliban political order,[8] many Iranian actions run counter to their own commitments and declarations of cooperation. Iranian security services did not adhere to the promises of Iranian diplomats engaging their Western counterparts.

Iranian strategy differs across regions. In Western Afghanistan and Herat, the Iranian government is implementing its Hezbollah, supporting proxies while seeking to monopolize the social service net. After the fall of the Taliban, Tehran dispatched Hasan Kazemi Qomi, a Revolutionary Guard commander who served as the Iranian regime's chief liaison to Hezbollah in Lebanon, as its chief "diplomat" in Herat.[9] He oversaw distribution of aid and projects ranging from road construction to power generation in the province.[10]

As U.S. forces consolidated control in Afghanistan, Iranian authorities worked to solidify their predominant influence, at least in Western Afghanistan. While the Iranian government contributed personnel to the reconstruction effort, for example, sending Persian-speaking schoolteachers to Herat, they used the dispatch of such volunteers to provide cover for Revolutionary Guardsmen and intelligence operatives. On March 8, 2002, Afghan commanders intercepted 12 Iranian agents and proxies who were organizing armed resistance among Afghan commanders.[11] Around the same time, the Iranian government's Dari-language radio

---

6 Ayatollah Ruhollah Khomeini (Hamid Algar, trans.), *Islam and Revolution*, London: Keegan Paul International, 1985, pp. 301, 323.

7 *9/11 Commission Report: Final Report of the National Commission on Terrorist Attacks Upon the United States*, New York: W. W. Norton, 2004, pp. 169, 240–241.

8 James Dobbins. "How to Talk to Iran," *Washington Post*, July 22, 2007, p. B7.

9 Ali Nourizadeh, "Iran Makes Last Minute Delegation Change Before US Meeting," *Asharq al-Awsat* (London), May 29, 2007.

10 "Iran Envoy Lists Iranian Infrastructure Projects in Afghan Herat Province," *Islamic Republic News Agency*, October 27, 2003.

11 Douglas Jehl, "A Nation Challenged: Outside Influences," *New York Times*, March 9, 2002, p. 10.

broadcasting into Afghanistan grew sharply more anti-American,[12] and Iranian support for former warlord patron and Herat governor Ismail Khan's resistance to the central government increased.[13] In March 2004, the Afghan National Army had to deploy its forces to Herat to rein in Ismail Khan; more than 100 people died in the ensuing battle. As a consolation, President Hamid Karzai appointed him Minister of Energy.

Iranian strategy goes beyond just the Hezbollah model's provision of social services, however. Iranian aid projects have consciously tied Western Afghanistan closer to Iran and away from Kabul. Western Afghanistan, for example, has become an extension of Iran's electrical grid rather than a cohesive part of the Afghanistan national grid. Likewise, Iranian transportation assistance favors road and even railroad projects that link Herat to the major cities of eastern Iran rather than major Afghan centers.[14]

Many other regional powers also seek to play out their interest in Afghanistan, although not necessarily to the same extent. Pakistan, though, has maneuvered to maintain predominant influence in eastern portions of Afghanistan, and, indeed, the history of its interventions since the 1950s has been geared to containing any spillover of Pushtun nationalism into Pakistan.[15] However, in the wake of the Taliban's fall, Pakistani security services have been either less successful or less methodical than have the Iranians in Western Afghanistan at imposing influence or using infrastructure to undercut the cohesiveness of the rebuilt Afghanistan republic.

The Iranian leadership is pragmatic, perhaps even more so than other regional players such as Pakistan, India, or Russia. It does not limit itself to a single coreligionist or ethnic proxy. While it used established clients such as Ismail Khan to further its predominance in Western Afghanistan, its outreach extends throughout Afghanistan. That Iranian policymakers now also provide support to their former Taliban enemies should not surprise.

Pragmatism in Practice: Outreach to the Taliban

The Iranian leadership is applying strategies developed in Lebanon and Iraq to Afghanistan. Iranian aggression and support for the Afghan insurgency appear correlated to its success in Iraq. Whereas Iranian officials once were cautious in the face of the proximity of so many American troops, repeated declarations from a bipartisan array of U.S. congressmen and senators has transformed what had been America's greatest strategic asset into a liability. The more U.S. policymakers reflect a desire to withdraw troops, the greater advantage the Islamic Republic can draw from keeping them occupied. Not only does low- or medium-level insurgency erode domestic U.S. support for its political leadership, but it also drains resources and constrains future military options. On July 30, 2007, for example, Iranian Foreign Minister

---

12 Bill Samii, "Mashhad Broadcasting Changes Its Tune," *Radio Free Europe/Radio Liberty (RFE/RL) Iran Report*, Vol. 5, No. 21, June 10, 2002.

13 Bill Samii, "Herat and Iran Strengthen Ties," *Radio Free Europe/Radio Liberty (RFE/RL) Iran Report*, July 8, 2002.

14 I draw upon the as-yet unpublished work and observations of my AEI colleague Frederick W. Kagan for this paragraph.

15 Barnett Rubin, *Fragmentation of Afghanistan: State Formation and Collapse in the International System*, New Haven, Conn.: Yale University Press, 1995, pp. 63–64.

Manouchehr Mottaki commented that the United States "is not in a position to get into a new military conflict."[16]

The similarities between Iranian policy toward Iraq and Afghanistan are evident in Iranian rhetoric. Mohammad-Ebrahim Taherian, Afghanistan coordinator in the Iranian foreign ministry, cited over 300 development projects—a chief component of the Hezbollah strategy—but then cited a theme common in Iranian pronouncements about Iraq. "While Iran contributes to development plans and security in Afghanistan," he said, "the presence of certain countries in this country has caused insecurity for the Afghan people,"[17] alluding to the allegedly destabilizing impact of the U.S. presence. The rhetoric of former President 'Ali Akbar Hashemi Rafsanjani in his statements about Afghanistan also holds eerie parallels to themes of U.S. weakness and loss that Iranian officials earlier projected with regard to the U.S. presence in Iraq. "The U.S. forces have no security in Afghanistan and have failed to materialize their declared objectives in that country," he said in an official weekly sermon, adding, "In Lebanon they had to accept a disgraceful defeat but still try to harm the oppressed movement of Hezbollah."[18]

Iraq has become a laboratory. Iranian-supported militias and terrorist groups exploit vulnerabilities in Afghanistan that corollary militias or insurgent groups identify in their attacks on U.S. forces in Iraq. Whereas the Iraqi insurgency was once limited to the periphery of that country, terrorist groups and militias made a conscious decision to take the fight to Baghdad, where, arguably, the U.S. presence was strongest. The Taliban now replicate that decision, seeking to move their fight from the mountains along the Pakistani border to Kabul itself.[19]

That the Taliban insurgency is gaining ground is undisputed. Whereas in Iraq, Iranian-backed militias exploited different rules of engagement between Coalition forces, in Afghanistan, the Taliban are quick to direct attacks on those NATO members, such as the Swedes and Germans, whose presence is more for political show than military effectiveness. But Taliban resurgence and imitation of successful tactics elsewhere is not proof of Iranian support.

Evidence of active Iranian involvement derives from intercepted Iranian arms shipments to the Taliban,[20] as well as exploitation of captured documents and interrogation of middlemen. Assumptions that such aid and assistance is impossible given the sectarian divide and historical animosity between Iran and the Taliban are misplaced. While U.S. officials like to cite Islamic Republic pragmatism as a reason why Iranian officials could overcome their animosity to the United States and strike a deal, pragmatism can go both ways: Tehran might also strike deals with other historic adversaries to stymie Washington.

This is not to claim that Iranian intelligence or Revolutionary Guards are the major force behind the Taliban: They are not. The Taliban is entrenched along Afghanistan's ill-defined and ill-accepted border with Pakistan. From its very inception, Pakistani Islamists in the army and Inter-Services Intelligence agency (ISI) have assisted if not enabled the Taliban. But the assumptions that proxy warfare in Afghanistan is clear-cut, with states lining up behind single

---

16 "Iran Rules Out US Attack," Fars News Agency (Tehran), July 30, 2007.

17 "Iran for Development, Security in Afghanistan," *IRNA*, May 28, 2007.

18 "Rafsanjani: World Should Admire Iran's Nuclear Achievements," *IRNA*, July 13, 2007.

19 "Taleban 'Shifting Focus to Kabul,' BBC News, June 21, 2007.

20 "US: 'Irrefutable' Proof Iran Arms Taliban," CBS News, June 13, 2007.

proxies, and that Iranian pragmatism does not extend to support for sectarian or ideological groups, which, on their surface, espouse ideologies inimical to Tehran, is naïve.

The Iranian leadership does not subject its allies to a sectarian litmus test. The Islamic Republic backs Christian Armenia against Shi'a Azerbaijan. The first foreign official whom Khomeini received after the Revolution was Palestinian Liberation Organization chairman Yasir Arafat, at the time a Sunni Marxist. Iranian officials support both Hamas and Palestinian Islamic Jihad, both militantly Sunni. Indeed, they founded the latter group. To reach out to the Taliban should not stretch credibility, especially if the goal of such Iranian assistance is more to bog the United States and NATO down and less to see the Taliban reassert dominance over Afghanistan.

Conclusion

Many U.S. diplomats assume that when a state teeters on failure, its neighbors will automatically seek its stability. The Baker-Hamilton Commission, for example, based its policy recommendation to engage Iran over the future of Iraq upon such a supposition. Such assumptions are wrong. They misread an Iranian strategy that affects U.S. interests not only in Iraq, but also in Afghanistan. The Iranian regime will accept stability in both its war-torn neighbors, but only under its terms. Barring that, Tehran believes controlled instability to be its next best option. Low- and mid-level insurgency not only neutralizes American strength and blocks the consolidation of liberal ideologies that might spread to threaten Iran theocracy, but also provides Iran with greater space to maneuver. For Iran, such a strategy requires not only exploiting historical links to Western Afghanistan, but also forming broader alliances against the U.S. interests and allies in the region, even if this means outreach to the Taliban. It is ironic that, as Iranian authorities prove their pragmatism and replicate strategies in Afghanistan that have worked in Iraq and Lebanon, rigid thinking in the West blinds many policymakers to the extent of possible Iranian subterfuge.

CHAPTER 4

Afghanistan and the Boomerang Effect

Mikkel Vedby Rasmussen[1]

In November 2006, I was walking around Kabul Airport with the members of an official Danish delegation as we tried to kill time until the Royal Danish Air Force C-130 waiting on the tarmac was ready to take us back to Europe. While the members of parliament bought carpets and fur coats, I went to a little shop that sold medals, coins, and other memorabilia that history had washed up in this part of the world. These coins and medals told the history of military intervention in Afghanistan. There were coins made in British India and campaign medals issued for Soviet soldiers. Some of the Soviet medals were brand-new, as if the Red Army had just left these symbols of its glory behind without bothering to present them to any soldier in the withdrawal of 1989. There were all sorts of memorabilia from armies that, in one way or another, had lost their way in Afghanistan. Leaving the souvenir shop, I was wondering whether some guy was going to come there in 15 or 20 years and look at ISAF medals, Euro coins, or whatever the current inhabitants of Kabul Airport might leave behind and have a quiet laugh at how these have been added to the collection of memorabilia from armies who have lost their way in Afghanistan.

The weight of history lies heavy on the shoulders of any soldier venturing into Afghanistan, and I believe that we are going to have to take a look at what the legacy of the current mission is going to be—in other words, how and under what circumstances the NATO and American missions are going to end. And we must do so in order to be able to assess what needs to be done now, and what the possibilities for success are going to be. Some may find this discussion defeatist. In many places where I have raised the issue of an 'exit strategy,' people look at me in disbelief at the mere notion of actually leaving. Everyone seems to agree that we are in Afghanistan for ten to 15 years. And when you visit people in Afghanistan, they will tell you that this is a long-term commitment and that we will have to stay there for a long time. But the fact is that we are not going to stay there for a long time.

Of course, USAID, the Danish development aid agencies, and the various NGOs are going to stay in Afghanistan until the end of time, but the military commitment is not going to last ten years. In fact, the troops are probably going to be withdrawn a lot quicker than that. So, the questions that remain are: What are we going to leave behind and how is the Afghani-

[1] Mikkel Vedby Rasmussen is the Head of the Danish Institute for Military Studies. He has previously worked at the Danish Institute for International Studies and at the Department of Political Science, University of Copenhagen. At present, his research focuses on how the security policies of Western societies are changing because these societies gradually are becoming 'risk societies'. Rasmussen would like to thank Peter Dahl Thruelsen from the Royal Danish Defence College as well as his colleagues at the Danish Institute for Military Studies for our discussions on Western strategy in Afghanistan, in addition to Peter Münster for his research assistance.

stan mission going to influence us and especially NATO? These questions, put together, sum up the European perspective that I would like to talk about today.

One way to answer these questions is to analyze Western, and especially European, policy in Afghanistan, in terms of 'the boomerang effect'. The sociologist Ulrich Beck coined this term, and he argues that we live in what he calls a 'risk' society: a society where we are always faced with the consequences of our own actions. Perhaps pollution is the best examples of this.[2] We simply cannot have a modern society without polluting, and, in return, we always end up facing the consequences of our own pollution. The consequences of our actions become a risk in their own right. This means, as Beck and others argue, that risk becomes inherent in action. People know very well that opening a factory creates pollution, and pollution simply becomes part of the equation. So dealing with the risk of acting becomes a pivotal part of policy: You do something and are stuck with the consequences.

This boomerang effect has three elements: Firstly, the identification of risk that results in the boomerang effect. Secondly, risk cultures that regard risk in different ways and therefore lead to different boomerang effects, and lastly, the question of risk compensation, which I will deal with in detail later on. For now, I will discuss the identification of risk and how this applies in a NATO context.

The Identification of Risk

The Secretary General is quite clear about the importance of the mission in Afghanistan. He says: 'Success in Afghanistan is of course of key importance for the positive answer to the question "Can the alliance deliver?"'[3] In other words, if NATO fails in Afghanistan, then NATO fails in general. The entire organization has been placed on the table when it comes to this mission. This follows a tradition within the alliance of always staking the alliance itself on some development goal. If you analyze NATO speeches since 1948, you will probably find that some kind of phrase meaning 'NATO is going to collapse if we don't do X' has been there all along. And whether it was about nuclear weapons, détente, the enlargement of NATO, deployable forces, capabilities of any kind, governments always put the alliance at stake—like a gambler that has run out of money and throws his car keys into the game. And it actually works. A bit dangerous perhaps, but it works. NATO seems to drive home in its own car almost every time.

As poker players know, putting your car or house at stake makes a lot more sense when sitting at the table than it does afterwards. When you sit there, you are certain that the next card will be the lucky one. Your wife, on the other hand, is probably not as thrilled at the probability of riding her bike for the rest of the year. And this is exactly what has been happening to NATO. The identification of the risk of the alliance has actually caught some member states by surprise, because at a meeting in Brussels it makes a lot of sense declaring that 'the Afghanistan mission is important, otherwise we will fail', but going back home and telling the

---

[2] Ulrich Beck (Mark Ritter, trans.), *Risk Society: Towards a New Modernity*, London: Sage Publications, 1992, p. 37. I have elaborated on the 'boomerang effect' and other elements of risk strategy in my *The Risk Society at War* (Cambridge, UK: Cambridge University Press, 2006).

[3] Speech by NATO Secretary General, Jaap de Hoop Scheffer at the Munich Conference of Security Policy, Munich, Germany, February 9, 2007, §2.

Italian electorate that they need to send troops to Afghanistan, telling the Germans that they will actually need to do some more fighting, is a different matter. The Afghanistan mission is not as important in Berlin, Rome, or Madrid as it is in Brussels—or in Helmand. And for that reason, betting the Alliance on this mission is proving very dangerous, because the players are not actually in the game, they are just saying so. And one of the reasons for this is the existence of different risk cultures.

Risk Cultures

People look a risk differently. Some people find river rafting something pleasant to do on weekends, whereas others might be scared to death just thinking about being in a small boat on a quiet lake. Governments also think differently about the risks entailed in this mission. They also think differently about what the mission is all about, and a lot of differences in perceptions can be taken back to the fact that they perceive the risks of the Afghanistan mission differently. When you read and when you listen to what European governments are actually telling their electorates, and even their armed forces, that this mission is all about, you sometimes have difficulties believing that this is actually all about the same one country. Some governments portray this as a primarily military mission—if you ask the Canadians, the Dutch, the Brits, or the Danes, this is about war fighting. Others see it rather as a development mission—the Swedes and the Germans believe they are doing development. Others, again, might combine the two, arguing that it is about a comprehensive approach to have military and civilian means at the same time, but there is no clear agreement on what is actually going on. And when you look at the rules of engagement given from individual governments to their individual contributions, it becomes very clear that they are not fighting the same war and that they do not even agree whether it is in fact a war that they are fighting or not.

These differences are also found within governments. The ministry of foreign affairs, the agencies responsible for aid, the military, and so on have very different conceptions of how to go about it. And when you have different conceptions of what the mission is all about and how each agency is going to take on the mission, then you should not be surprised at the fact that there are different risk assessments involved. If you are in fact on a development mission, you simply do not expect to get shot at; if you are on a military mission, you find the risk of being shot at, as well as shooting other people, an inherent part of what you are doing. So because different nations and different agencies have different risk cultures, they simply do not agree on what they should be doing and they are not doing the same things. So, what happens if you do things differently, but you perceive that you are doing the right thing while others have misunderstood what this is all about? The result is resentment. Unfortunately, a very normal thing between people of different cultures, no one seems to understand why one person is doing one thing while another person is doing something completely different. Cultures are incommensurable. At the moment, NATO is trying to create a compromise from different cultures, a compromise that simply does not exist. You might be able to paint over the differences, but you cannot make them go away. At some point the alliance will have to make a choice of what kind of mission it is and what kind of risks it entails. But this is a choice nowhere close to being made yet, and because of that there is a great uncertainty within the alliance of what this is all about. And this uncertainty has its own boomerang effect. It creates the sense within the alliance that the mission is lost, which in turn further undermines the commitment to carry it on.

And this is not good at all, because at some point being risk-averse becomes a risk in itself. NATO must in fact perform, just in order to show that it can. In order to show the people of Europe that the alliance is actually an effective security organisation, it needs to prevail in Afghanistan. And in order to show the Taliban, or whomever the opposition in Afghanistan might consist of, that NATO is an effective force, it has to take risks out there, in other words risking soldiers' lives, in order to be able to show that it is actually able to do some real war fighting. This has been the case for individual troop deployments, for instance, when the Danes arrived in southern Afghanistan they were clearly tested by the local Taliban commander, trying to find out whether these guys could actually fight. And they could, so the Taliban changed their strategy. But it is also true on the national level for all of Afghanistan that NATO will have to prove its worth in order to be able to say to these people that we can produce results.

So, NATO will have to take risks, with the boomerang effects that this entails, in order to be effective. And this is why talking of leaving is not in some way betraying the mission. To discuss exit strategies is not to undermine the troops. Because there is no one more concerned about what the exit strategy is going to look like than the Taliban on the one hand and the Afghan government on the other. They would actually rather like to know, because what really scares them is the risk of NATO just cutting and running. And one illustration of how the international Islamist networks are very conscious is the letter to Abu Musaf al-Zarqawi, where Zawahiri of Al Qaeda wrote to him: "Things may develop faster than we imagined. The aftermath of the collapse of American power in Vietnam and how they ran and left the agents is noteworthy". He was writing about Iraq, but he could easily have been writing about Afghanistan. What is very well known in the opposition is the fact that western governments withdraw. So in order to have a coherent strategy, you need to have a strategy for withdrawal. You need to show what your end points are, how you are going to achieve them, and how strong your commitments are to them. Otherwise you risk the mission itself.

Risk Compensation

The third element of the boomerang effect is risk compensation. A good example of this is the use of seatbelts. Many of the analyses done on the introduction of seatbelt laws in most western countries in the 1970s actually show that forcing people to use seatbelts actually increases the number of accidents. People involved in the accidents benefit from seatbelts, but it seems that more accidents occur in countries that have introduced mandatory seatbelts—because people risk compensate. They know that they will not be hurt all that much when they crash in their car, so they crash in their car.[4] And security policy works in similar ways. It does so on a strategic level as well as on a tactical level.

Risk compensation on the strategic level is something we have seen since the end of the cold war. The increased number of military interventions and the belief in the effectiveness and surgical nature of military power is a case of risk compensation. The West can prevail in conflicts of our time primarily because of technological superiority. The costs of fighting are

[4] John Adams, *Risk,* London: Routledge, 1995, pp. 113–34.

low, therefore there is a tendency to fight more and be more ambitious in your war-fighting goals. And then we have the risks. Risk compensation is exactly what has been going on in Afghanistan. It started out as a mission with a very limited mandate. The Americans' ambitions back when the conflict started was merely to get rid of the Taliban and to kill as many terrorists involved in 9-11 as possible. There were very specific levels for how many troops were to be introduced. The Pentagon was very conscious about not being ambitious, but gradually the mission took on a logic of its own and the ambitions were increased—people began talking about introducing democracy in Afghanistan. Thus development became an important part of the mission, and suddenly we found ourselves in a project of nation-building. Obviously, the risks involved in trying to introduce a modern democracy in a society such as Afghanistan's are somewhat larger than if you just want to make sure that the right government is in place in Kabul. So, the increased ambitions have increased the level of risks, and this is also true on the tactical level.

The Western forces are still not numerous on the ground and thus they rely to a very large extent on air power. Air power becomes their 'tactical seatbelt'. The result is that in some places we are fighting a very high-intensity campaign at a moment when winning hearts and minds and building up society is also important, and combining the two is very difficult indeed. Again, further risks develop and you end up dropping bombs on villages you would actually have liked to have on your side.

This brings me back to the souvenir shop in Kabul Airport. Will there, sometime in the future, in fact be a soldier from a Chinese peacekeeping force, standing where I stood, looking at ISAF memorabilia and having a quiet laugh about the time when European soldiers tried to bring stability and democracy to Afghanistan? This question cannot be answered with any degree of certainty at the moment, but perhaps the real legacy of this mission is not to be found in Kabul, but in Brussels. Because NATO has put the existence of the alliance itself on the table when it comes to this mission, it is hard to underestimate the effects that the Afghanistan mission is going to have on NATO. I believe that we are witnessing a boomerang effect, where NATO for political reasons within the alliance has made this mission more important than perhaps it should have been. We should remind ourselves that NATO is always talking about the demise of the alliance, and for that reason one should always take these discussions with the proper amount of skepticism. As long as the discussion exists, however, NATO's capability to act in Afghanistan is the defining debate of the alliance. And so, the risks of the mission are the risks of the alliance's continued existence. And any reform agenda in NATO, whether it is about creating a new command structure or about the operability of the NRF, all of this is going to be viewed from an outcome perspective. But the implication of this is, of course, and this is perhaps the final and most real boomerang effect from a NATO perspective, is that this fight in Afghanistan is not about Afghanistan. It is about NATO. And much of what NATO is doing is due to the internal politics of the alliance rather than what is needed on the ground. So to succeed in Afghanistan, one needs to succeed in Brussels. And in order to succeed in Brussels, one will need to take account of the different risk cultures, one will need to take risk compensation into account, and one will need to deal with the boomerang effect. The best way to do this is to have a number of clear and coherent goals that together define the moment when NATO can actually declare mission accomplished.

CHAPTER 5

Hokumat Versus *Yaghistan*: The Historical Challenge of State/Tribe Conflict to State Building in Afghanistan

Ali Alfoneh[1]

The vast territory that is now covered within the international borders of modern-day Afghanistan is an ancient land belonging to an ancient civilization. The Afghan state, on the other hand, is relatively young, its history usually traced back to the mid-18th century. As in most other young states, building a sovereign, and one might add modern, centralized state in Afghanistan—at the very least since the reigns of Abdur Rahman Khan (r. 1880–1901) and most certainly Amanullah Khan (r. 1919–1929)—has been the ultimate goal of most if not all Afghan rulers. This includes not only the Marxist political elites of the Democratic Republic of Afghanistan (1978–1992) and the Taleban regime (1996–2001) but also the ultimate goal of the Islamic Republic of Afghanistan under the presidency of Hamed Karzai (interim President 2002–2004; elected President since 2004).

Despite the focus of this seminar on Afghanistan today and the challenges to state building in the contemporary era, I respectfully suggest a historical approach. Resistance to state building efforts in Afghanistan is not a new phenomenon, and indeed all Afghan rulers have faced formidable challenges in their state building and centralization efforts. In other words, experiences from the past could provide valuable insights and suggestions to the methods and mechanics of state building today.

In its softer forms, resistance to state building manifests itself as bribing representatives of the state; isolation of officials from contact with the life of the villages; and penetration of the ranks of the bureaucracy to divert public funds and money to the benefit of the tribe. But at times, it also manifests itself in the form of major regional conflicts. The four "civil wars", six revolts, and a large number of local insurrections during the 21-year reign of Abdur Rahman Khan (r. 1880–1901) serve as examples of such challenges.[2] Resistance also manifests itself in the form of *Jihad*, or "Holy War", being either declared in order to protect the periphery from encroachment by the center, or as a direct attempt at gaining the ultimate prize, state power and the treasures of the capital. The revolt against Amanullah Khan (r. 1919–1929)

1 Ali Alfoneh is a research fellow at the Institute for Strategy, Royal Danish Defence College, in Denmark. His research interests include civil military relations in North Africa and the Middle East and Iran.

2 For a complete account of the internal warfare waged by Abdur Rahman Khan, see his fascinating autobiography: Abdur Rahman (Mir Munshi, ed.), *The Life of Abdur Rahman*, London: John Murray, 1990, Vol. I, Chapter 10.

in 1928–1929[3] and the war against the Soviet-backed Democratic Republic of Afghanistan (1978–1992)[4] serve as prime examples of this phenomenon.

But, regardless of their garbs, resistance to state building efforts in Afghanistan emanates from a much deeper source of conflict: The conflict between center and periphery, or *hokumat* [where governing takes place] and *yaghistan* [the lands of freedom or unrestraint]. This hypothesis is derived from the neoclassics of Afghanology, mainly from the American anthropologist Jon W. Andersen;[5] the great French Afghanologue Olivier Roy's notion of "separation" between state and society;[6] and more precisely the American diplomat scholar Leon B. Poullada, who coins it: "[T]he conflict between state power and tribal power in the traditional Afghan polity" or more simply: "The central government [which attempts] to impose its authority and the centrifugal forces of a tribal society [...]."[7]

I tend to see some of the difficulties of the present Afghan administration in the same light as resistance to state building in earlier historical experiences. The very same centrifugal forces of the traditional society, which constituted insurmountable obstacles to state building and centralization in earlier attempts at state building, also risk to derail democratic state building of the Karzai administration.

In this attempt I suggest some comments on three attempts at state building: Ahmad Shah and Abdul Rahman Khan's gradual approach to state building, and Amanullah Khan's state building as a cultural revolution from above (not much unlike the Marxist cultural revolution from above to come).

The first question arising for any student of Afghan history is the simple question of what conditions shaped the Afghan in the first place despite the centrifugal forces of the tribal society? The literature stresses that the appearance of an independent Afghan political entity was only possible because of the political vacuum created by the disintegration of the Persian and Mughal empires, the immediate reason being the assassination of the Persian King Nader Shah Afshar on June 9, 1747. A warrior leading the Durrani mercenaries in the armies of Nader, Ahmad Shah (r. 1747–1772) of the Abdali (later called Durrani) tribe had made a great name for himself as a warrior.

After the assassination of Nader, Ahmad Shah escaped to Afghanistan with most of Nader's treasure and had gold and a reputation that bought him the support of Durrani tribal chiefs.[8] A *Jirga*, or tribal council of Pashtun chiefs, was formed in 1747 in order to elect a "paramount chief by the chieftains of the subtribes and clans of the Abdali tribe."[9] The election was closely contested by the more powerful clans and, as the Afghan chronicler Kohzad correctly

[3] For the best account of the revolt against Amanullah, see Leon B. Poullada, *Reform and Rebellion in Afghanistan, 1919–1929,* Ithaca: Cornell University Press, 1973. For a more recent account in Persian, see K. Pamir Peykar, *Zohour va Soghout-e A'la-Hazrat Amanullah Khan* [The Rise and Fall of His Majesty Amanullah Khan] Toronto: Pegah, 2003.

[4] For a comprehensive account of the *Jihad* see Olivier Roy, *Islam and Resistance in Afghanistan.* Cambridge, UK: Cambridge University Press, 1986.

[5] Jon W. Anderson, "Khan and Khel: Dialectics of Pakhtun Tribalism," in Richard Tapper, ed., *The Conflict of Tribe and State in Iran and Afghanistan.* London, Canberra, and New York: Croom Helm & St. Martin's Press, 1983, p. 125.

[6] Roy (1986, p. 10)

[7] Poullada (1973, pp. 6, 28).

[8] Poullada (1973, p. 2).

[9] Poullada (1973, p. 1).

points out: "Ahmad Shah's greatest asset was the fact that the powerful clans could agree on a member of a weak clan, who would lack a strong tribal base of his own and would have to court the good will of the chiefs of the more powerful elements."[10] Therefore, a combination of Ahmad Shah's treasure, reputation, and intra-tribal struggles for power facilitated his election as "*Padeshah* [King] of the Afghans" in 1747.[11]

The tribal confederation (*ulus*), led by Ahmad Shah, was an instrument of rationalizing and improving tribal warfare. This enterprise was, in the words of the French Afghanologue Olivier Roy, held together by "the common aim of conquering neighbouring areas with a view to pillaging or exacting tribute."[12] The founding tribes of the Afghan state were exempted from taxation, and the state's resources expanded as a result of conquest of fertile agricultural areas rather than economic growth. According to one study, over three-fourths of the state's income came from Ahmad Shah's conquests in India, mainly Punjab and Kashmir, not from the provinces that today compose Afghanistan.[13] Ahmad Shah pursued this bold expansionist policy with the support of the Pashtun tribes and their hereditary royal officer corps.[14]

In other words, in its original form, the traditional "social contract" between the Afghan tribes and the Afghan state consisted of the responsibility of the tribes to deliver tribal warriors under arms (*lashkar*) in exchange for a share in the material benefits and glory.[15] The tribes considered the state responsible for the administration of new territories conquered by the tribal confederation. But, "[a]s far as [tribal] territory [was] concerned, the presence of the state would seem to be redundant and totally unnecessary."[16] Thus, the existence of the parallel realms of the state and the tribe secured the early phase of state formation in Afghanistan.

While most Afghan chroniclers call Ahmad Shah "Ahmad Shah Baba", meaning "father of the nation", it was the "Iron Amir", Sardar Abdur Rahman Khan (r. 1880–1901) who kept Russia and Britain at arm's length, gradually weakened the power of the tribes, and institutionalized the bureaucracy and the Afghan army.

Thomas Hobbes emphasized three centuries ago that the inability of the government to instill awe is decisive for the occurrence of rebellions,[17] and Abdur Rahman most certainly proved awe-inspiring. With the newly established conscript Afghan army as his ultimate source of power, the Amir ruthlessly crushed the revolts he was facing, among them dynastic claims by his cousins, but he also managed to annex to his realm territories that had remained virtually independent, such as the Shi'ite Hazarjat in 1891 and the non-Islamic Kafiristan in 1896,

---

[10] Ali Ahmad Kohzad, *Men and Events through Eithteenth and Nineteenth Century Afghanistan*, Kabul: Historical Society of Afghanistan, no date. Quoted in Poullada (1973, p. 2).

[11] Daniel Balland, "X. Political History," in Ehsan Yarshater, ed., *Encyclopædia Iranica, Vol. 1*, London: Routledge and Kegan Paul; Costa Mesa, Calif.: Mazda, 1985.

[12] Roy (1986, p. 13).

[13] Yuri Gankovsky, "The Durrani Empire: Taxes and Tax System, State Incomes and Expenditure," in Social Sciences Today Editorial Board, eds., *Afghanistan Past and Present*, Moscow: USSR Academy of Sciences, 1981, p. 90. Quoted in Barnett R. Rubin, "Lineages of the State in Afghanistan," *Asian Survey*, No. 28, 1988, p. 1192.

[14] Balland (1985).

[15] Roy (1986, pp. 13–14).

[16] Roy (1986, p. 14).

[17] Thomas Hobbes, *Leviathan*. London: Everyman's Library, 1914, p. 1651.

which he renamed Nurestan (land of light) after forced conversions of the inhabitants.[18] The conscript army also enhanced the central government's ability to extract tax revenues from land owners.[19]

Abdur Rahman's success was partly due to his political ability, but also to financial support and arms given by England to stabilize Afghanistan as a buffer state between British India and Imperial Russia. By constructing strategic roads, bridges, and caravansaries all serving to expand the outreach of central government even to the remotest areas of the realm; ordering forced migrations; building an internal spy network; and appointing provincial governors, he managed to strengthen the state.[20] In his own words, his task was one of putting "in order all those hundreds of petty chiefs, plunderers, robbers and cutthroats. . . . This necessitated breaking down the feudal and tribal system and substituting one grand community under one law and one rule."[21] The Amir thus left a consolidated state to his eldest son, who succeeded to the throne peacefully upon his father's natural death.

While Abdur Rahman's gradual state building efforts led the foundations of modern Afghanistan, it is King Amanullah (r. 1919–1929) who attempted to catapult Afghanistan into the 20th century. Amanullah came to power after the assassination of his father, Amir Hbibullah Khan (1901–1919), in Jalalabad, and swiftly moved against his uncle, Nasrullah Khan, the head of the traditionalist clergy *(ulema)* and tribal faction whom he charged with the responsibility of the assassination.[22] At this very early stage, Amanullah risked alienating the traditionalists, but his independent policies managed to mobilize the traditional forces of Afghan society. Addressing the people of Afghanistan, Amanullah expressed his gratitude to the "honorable nation of Afghanistan" for "putting the crown of the Kingdom" on his head, and granted all citizens complete freedom and safety from "all forms of oppression and transgression" and promised that all citizens would be "subject to the law." The keywords of his coronation speech set the tone of his entire rule: consultation (*Shura*), faith (*din*), state (*dawlat*), nation (*millat*), and motherland (*watan*).[23]

Amanullah's promises of total national independence for the country led to his declaration of *Jihad* against the British, or the Third Anglo-Afghan War (1919). In the wake of the Great War there was little enthusiasm for war among British troops. Therefore, Afghanistan was granted independence, and Amanullah became not only a national hero, but a Pan Islamist hero of an Islamic civilization subjugated to European colonial rule.[24] But Afghanistan's

---

[18] For an exhaustive account of Abdur Rahman's campaigns, see Rahman (1990, Vol. I, Chapter 10). See also M. Hasan Kakar, *Government and Society in Afghanistan—The Reign of Amir Abd Al-Rahman Khan*, Austin: University of Texas Press, 1979.

[19] According to Kakar, "By 1891 the yearly revenue in the reign of Amir Abd al-Rahman had increased by slightly less than four times the revenue of the last year of the reign of Amir Shr Ali Khan [Abd-ur-Rahman's predecessor]" (Kakar, 1979, p. 90).

[20] Louis Dupree, *Afghanistan*. Princeton, N.J.: Princeton University Press, 1980, p. 420.

[21] Rahman (1990).

[22] Vartan Gregorian, *The Emergence of Modern Afghanistan: Politics of Reform and Modernization, 1880–1946,* Stanford, Calif.: Stanford University Press, 1969, pp. 220–228.

[23] Amanullah, quoted in Mir-Muhammad Gholam Ghubar, *Afghanestan dar Masir-e Tarikh* [Afghanistan in the Course of History], Mayvand, 2004, p. 752.

[24] Amanullah was even considered worthy of the title of Khalif after the Turkish President Mustafa Kemal Ataturk's abolishment of the Khalifat on March 3, 1924.

declaration of independence from Britain also meant the loss of British political and military support against Russian and subsequently Soviet imperial designs; annual subsidies and arms had been an important source of internal security since 1880.[25]

More importantly, as pointed out by the Afghan scholar Professor Nazif Shahrani, Amanullah's revision of the Pan Islamist policies of the past, establishment of correct relations with the Soviet Union, and abandonment of the "Muslim cause" in Russian Central Asia brought him the resentment of the traditionalist clergy and peoples of Northern Afghanistan. In the South, Amanullah's revised and correct policies towards the British made him enemies.[26] But it was Amanullah's accelerated attempt to centralize authority and radically transform the Afghan society from a traditional society into a modern one that led to rebellion. Amanullah's Western-inspired administrative, legal, social, economic, and political reforms, presented in three stages and some of which were declared but never truly implemented, were 20 years ahead of the ability of the Afghan society.[27] The symbolic attempts, such as removing the veil from the women, opening co-educational schools, and the attempt to force all Afghan in Kabul to wear Western clothing, and the more substantial attempt at subjugating the tribes into central control, all proved catastrophic for the radical modernizer. The dream palace of Amanullah collapsed after he returned from his much-celebrated tour in Europe, and the Pashtun tribesmen's revolt in Jalalabad in November 1928 set the entire tribal landscape alight. Both the Tajik and Pashtuns marched towards Kabul, and Amanullah had no choice but to flee.

Interestingly, some of the centralization and modernization efforts of Amanullah were also attempted by the Marxist regime in Afghanistan. Amanullah's nationalism turned into Marxist internationalism and rule of law turned into reign of terror. The Marxist cultural revolution from above ended, as was the case with Amanullah, in revolt of the tribal leaders and declaration *Jihad* against the central government. Amanullah's vision of Afghanistan was many years too soon for the Afghan society, and Marxist rule never managed to integrate the traditional sources of authority into the power structure of the state.

The Karzai administration faces some of the very same challenges that earlier rulers of Afghanistan did, and we should not be disheartened by the resistance it faces. But as opposed to earlier experiences, the Karzai administration has the benefit of a democratic foundation for reforms. And as the historical experience teaches us, a gradual state building process, rather than an attempt to revolutionize society, secures state building in a traditional polity. Integration of traditional structures of authority in the modern state could provide a better avenue for state building and secure the survival of the state beyond the foreign military presence in Afghanistan.

---

[25] Nazif M. Shahrani, "State Building and Social Fragmentation in Afghanistan—A Historical Perspective," in Ali Banuazizi and Myron Weiner, eds., *The State, Religion and Ethnic Politics. Afghanistan, Iran, and Pakistan*, New York: Syracuse University Press, 1986, p. 45.

[26] Shahrani (1986, p. 46).

[27] See Poullada (1973) on the three phases of the reforms and Dupree (1980) on the Afghan society unprepared for Amanullah's reforms.

CHAPTER 6

The Tribal Structure of Waziristan: Implications for Counterterrorism Policy in Afghanistan and Pakistan

Angel Rabasa[1]

This presentation describes work done at RAND to analyze the tribal structure of the Federally-Administered Tribal Areas of Pakistan (FATA) and assess the implications of the cultural, social, and political characteristics of Pashtun society in this region for counterterrorism policy in Afghanistan and Pakistan.

In conducting our research, we were confronted with very significant data-collection and analytical challenges. One challenge was the lack of up-to-date data. Many of the basic ethnographic sources dated back to the time of the British Raj. In keeping with the ways in which the British operated, Indian Army officers and various political agents wrote a number of "ethnographic" and biographical essays describing their individual experiences and the tribes and situations they encountered.

Upon independence, Pakistani political agents also wrote such memoirs and ethnographic studies of Waziristan that bore much similarity to those authored by the British. These efforts appear to have been rather intense in the 1980s and seem to have been precipitated by the Soviet invasion of Afghanistan and reflected Pakistan's security concerns on its western border.

In addition to field research in Pakistan, other sources are Pakistani censuses, data on socioeconomic indexes published by international organizations, and the Pakistani press, where more up-to-date information about the various tribes and their interactions with each other and with the central government can be obtained.

Almost all of the tribes in Waziristan are Pashtun. Inhabitants of the region speak an intermediate dialect of Pushto influenced by both the language's "hard" northern and "soft" southern dialects, respectively. The Wazirs migrated eastward to the region from the Khost area of Afghanistan in the fourteenth century and have long constituted the area's most important tribe.

The demarcation of the Durand line separating Afghanistan and the British Raj in the early 1890s left a small part of the Wazir tribe on the Afghan side of the border. In 1895, the British divided the region east of the Line in two, establishing the North Waziristan Agency (NWA) and the South Waziristan Agency (SWA). This division largely separated the two main branches of the Wazir tribe as well, with most of the Ahmedzai in SWA and most of the Utmanzai in NWA. The Mahsuds share a common ancestry with the Wazirs and make up the region's second-largest tribe. The Mahsuds are mostly in SWA. Three smaller tribes are present

---

1 Angel Rabasa is a senior policy analyst at the RAND Corporation who has written extensively about Islamic extremism, terrorism, and insurgency.

in SWA: the Suleman Khel and Dottani, which are both nomadic, though in the process of sedentarization, and the Urmur (or Burkis), a tribe believed to be indigenous to the region.

A History of Resistance to Central Authority

The tribes of the Federally Administered Tribal Areas (FATA), of which North and South Waziristan are part, have different histories with respect to resistance or cooperation with outside authorities. The Pashtuns of Waziristan have a particularly long history of military resistance. For 300 years, the tribes successfully fought off the Indian Mughal Empire and prevented its armies from entering Waziristan. Wazir, Mahsud, Daurs, and Bhattani tribes contributed enormously to the Durrani military when Ahmed Shah Durrani founded the Afghan state in 1747.

In 1849, the British took over the administration of the settled districts of Bannu and Dera Ismail Khan. Until 1860, the British left the Wazirs and Mahsuds pretty much alone. That year, Mahsud and Ahmedzai Wazir tribesmen attacked and looted the relatively prosperous provincial town of Tank, some 80 kilometers east of Wana, the main town of South Waziristan. In retaliation, British administrator Neville Chamberlain (no relation to the subsequent Prime Minister) undertook a punitive expedition into tribal territory.

In 1919, the Waziristan tribes briefly drove the British out of Wana. An estimated 2,200 soldiers and 43 British officers, as well as 4,000 tribesmen died in the fighting. Success in that war ultimately allowed Afghanistan's reformist king Amanullah to win sovereignty from Britain, thus making Afghanistan the first independent Muslim country of the twentieth century. In 1929, the tribes of Waziristan joined a Pashtun tribal army that marched on Kabul and deposed and killed Habibullah Kalkani, an ethnic Tajik insurgent who held Kabul's throne for nine months after overthrowing Manullah Khan.

Waziristan was also the stage of a full-scale war in 1936–1938, when Haji Mirzali Khan (popularly known as the Faqir of Ipi), a charismatic Muslim cleric, led a broad-based uprising against the British. In the 1930s, some 50,000 British troops were permanently stationed in Waziristan—more than all the other British troops stationed to the subcontinent combined.

Legal and Administrative Regime

While geographically part of Pakistan, the region has a distinct colonial-era legal and administrative system. The peculiar feature of the system—agency administration—is that tribesmen have been left to be governed by their customs and traditions. The colonial-era office of political agent, the representative of the central government, remains very powerful, at least in theory. The political agent combines the functions of a judge, magistrate, police chief, and civilian administrator. The Political Agent rules through a system of patron-client relations with the tribal leaders, known as maliks, and influential clerics. His authority is unchecked, and he is not answerable to any court. For instance, the political agent, or tribal area administrator, is empowered to imprison anybody for up to three years without due process of law.

The legal system in force in the tribal areas includes the concept of collective responsibility, which means that a whole tribe can be held responsible for the crimes of a single individual.

Of course, the authority of the political agents is circumscribed by the central government's ability to enforce its will in the face of powerful informal power structures.

Power Structure

There are two major power players within the Wazir tribal structure: the maliks (tribal elders) and the mullahs (religious functionaries). Historically, the key actor in tribal politics is the malik. He is almost always the key leader of a tribe, its section, or subsection and usually the most senior male. However, the authority of the malik is far from absolute. Unlike neighboring Pashtun tribes, there are no khans, walis, or nawabs in Waziristan. Hierarchy and rank are downplayed and deemphasized. A famous Wazir proverb states that every man is a malik.

During the colonial period, the British adopted a strategy of using tribal chiefs, and in those areas where chiefs did not exist, creating them. Loyal chiefs were given the official title of malik by the political agent. Official maliks gained political power, economic benefits, and social status. This colonial administration practice continues into the present day, and official maliks, with the passage of time, have grown wealthy through government patronage. They receive special benefits, such as the appointment of kin to the Khassadars or tribal levies, low-level government jobs, contracts for development projects, and a monthly stipend.

In return for these benefits, maliks are expected to assist the administration. Duties entail safeguarding the main road and helping the administration maintain state interests. In practice, this sort of indirect rule is more effective in the settled districts than it is in the tribal areas.

The imposition of a hierarchical political institution on a society with an egalitarian structure has created feelings of discontent and a degree of tension within the society and may be one of the factors that facilitated today's widespread and powerful Talibanization of the frontier region.

The other important political players are the mullahs. Historically, the mullah was subordinate to the malik. However, the anti-Soviet jihad in the 1980s fundamentally altered the political economy of the region by empowering the mullahs. Because of their contacts with donors from outside Waziristan, the mullahs gained access to arms and money with which to supply the Afghan mujahideen. As a result, over the past three decades, they have gone from being mostly poor village prayer leaders to powerful political players. In doing so, they have assumed a role of political leadership and contested the traditional wielders of power in tribal society, the maliks.

The current rise to power of the mullahs in Pashtun society has little to do with the realities of the society itself. Rather, it is more a product of the larger geopolitical situation of the region and the increasing power of Taliban and Al Qaeda elements. In times of war, the mullah has the ability to rally the tribal lashkar and proclaim jihad. In times of jihad, the mullah's power often overshadows that of the tribal elders. He is able to bypass the maliks and influence the tribal members directly. In this way, charismatic mullahs are able to monopolize power, mobilize society, and lead the struggle against the enemy. The rise of the mullahs is one of the factors that have led to erosion of the long-standing tribal preference for malik leaders.

During times of war, the mullah's power is limited by one crucial factor: whether or not the enemies are Muslim. In theory at least, battles against fellow Muslims cannot be considered a jihad, and as a result the mullah's role becomes superfluous. Indications of this can be seen in an episode during the conflict between the Taliban and the Northern Alliance. Tribesmen from Machikhel and Khwajadarkhel joined the jihad in Afghanistan at the urging of local clerics. Upon entering the war, they learned that their enemies were not infidels, but fellow Muslims from the Northern Alliance. As a result, many felt a sense of betrayal. On the other hand, radicals regularly stigmatize fellow Muslims as infidels (*kufar*), although most Sunni scholars in Pakistan believe that the practice of *takfir* (heretification) is in contradiction with the teachings of Islam.

Tribal members tend to follow the allegiance of their leaders. For example, if the leadership of a particular tribe is progovernment, on the main, the entire tribe will support this position. The tribal leader represents his people in a forum, which is more often than not, the tribal assembly or jirga. However, there are also exceptions to such norms: For instance, many individuals or families or clans might not agree to follow their leaders.

Pashtunwali: The Pashtun Code of Conduct

Pashtunwali, the code of honor of the Pashtuns, is prevalent amongst the tribes of Waziristan. Its primary injunction is to maintain honor and avoid shame (*sharm*). Most tribesmen will go to extreme lengths to avoid bringing shame upon themselves, their families, and their tribe or clan. (Note that the honor of a man is contingent on the honor of the women under his control.) Some scholars maintain that it is as much a "tribal law" as it is a code of honor and that it encompasses a wide range of Pashtun customs. It is the sum total of those ideals, meanings, and qualities required from a Pashtun or binding upon them. The key concepts of Pashtunwali are the following:

Melmastia (also *Hamsaya*). This is the notion of ideal, hospitable behavior that requires that any supplicant should enjoy the host's protection and should neither be harmed nor surrendered to an enemy.

Nanwatai refers to the idea of an enemy begging for forgiveness or protection; the term literally means "going along with the elders to the place of one's enemy." The person so seeking peace is expected to ritually humiliate himself in some way. This is supposed to elicit magnanimity in repayment for humiliation, leaving the offended party no option but to accept the petitioner's entreaty. Once the petitioner has humbled himself, tribal elders determine the size of the indemnity to be paid to the offended party. The offended party often refuses any compensation from the petitioner, offering the offender an unconditional pardon. Anything less is regarded as ungracious.

The adult male is to be maximally independent and not subject to the will of another. This is reflected in the emphasis given to "arriving at decisions on matters of concern by consensus in the jirga." Simultaneously, value is ascribed to the political independence of a tribe as a whole.

Badal (literally "exchange," figuratively "revenge") requires violent reaction to death, injury, and insult. Advances on one's *zan*, *zar*, or *zamin* ("women," "wealth," or "land") are the most common wrongs that require avenging, especially insults to women's sexual purity. The only successful defense of honor is revenge, equal to but not exceeding the original insult.

It is very important to remember that although there are some universal pillars of Pashtunwali, such as hospitality (*Melmastia*), revenge (*Badal*), and forgiveness (*Nanwatai*), the practice varies from tribe to tribe and region to region and that historically, there has been a degree of flexibility in the code.[2]

Today's talibanization of Waziristan has introduced the Taliban style code of conduct, which includes modern elements such as addition of Deobondi interpretations of Islam, Shia law, and the pan Islamic approach of Wahhabism.[3] Pashtunwali code has thus been weakened by both the introduction and practice of this "modern version" as well as a deterioration of tribal leadership under Taliban rule.

Attitudes Toward al Qaeda, the Taliban, and the United States

Before 2004, tribal groups showed flexibility toward Pakistani military incursions, but remained adamantly opposed to any operations by infidels. According to one account, "Tribals in this area decided in a traditional jirga that if the Pakistan army and paramilitary forces, with the help of tribal elders, launch any search operation, the locals will cooperate. But they do not like Americans in their area."[4] Indeed, many elders have turned over al Qaeda suspects to the government, but only on the condition that the accused would not be handed over to the United States.[5]

Tribal sentiments toward the Taliban and al Qaeda are more difficult to gauge. Many tribesmen formally professed admiration and even identification with al Qaeda and even more so with the Taliban, a sentiment that could be attributed to Pashtunwali. According to Pashtunwali, hospitality and honor are inextricably intertwined. Thus, the protection of al Qaeda fighters may reflect more of a cultural practice than ideological identification.

On the other hand, the operation of these factors may have been weakened by the fundamental shift away from tribalism that has taken place in Waziristan. This is the result of the large-scale destruction of the tribal structure by the Taliban (including the killing of key tribal leadership). This decreased autonomy has curbed the ability of tribal leaders to control or even monitor Taliban activity.[6] Any remaining hospitality can be seen in the local authority's collaboration with Taliban forces, which has inspired local leaders to "emulate the Taliban style rule."[7]

There are other complicating factors that are influencing the relationship between al Qaeda and the Waziri people. History has shown that the Pashtun tribesmen are extremely dif-

---

[2] For example, if someone is taking refuge in a home, and should this act of giving refuge bring problems to the host, that person is obliged to move on if he has other alternatives. Or if the tribal jirga has concluded that specific persons cannot be harbored, it is incumbent on them to take leave of their hosts. However, things become more difficult if the supplicant has no other alternatives. The host will not be inclined to turn this person out if he has nowhere to go. This may apply, in this case, to the wives and other female relatives of the so-called mujahideen. In fact, this notion of hospitality is so important in some areas that it even crosses religious boundaries. Sikhs and Hindus who have fled Afghanistan and have nowhere else to go have been given refuge in this area.

[3] Ahmed Rashid, *Taliban: The Story of the Afghan Warlords*, London: Pan Books, 2000, pp. 132, 139.

[4] "US Troops Not Welcome Here, Warn Pakistani Tribal Belt Residents," Agence France Press, August 28, 2002.

[5] Ismail Khan, "Crackdown Launched as Tribesmen Seek Time," *Dawn*, October 10, 2003.

[6] Seth G. Jones, "Pakistan's Tribal Deals Aren't Working," *International Herald Tribune*, December 28, 2006.

[7] International Crisis Group, *Pakistan's Tribal Areas: Appeasing the Militants*, Crisis Group Asia Report No. 125, December 2006.

ficult to intimidate. As one Wazir puts it, "Ask a Wazir politely to go to hell, he'll go. But push him to go to heaven, and he'll fight you to the death."[8] Any direct foreign military action will most likely provoke age-old defense mechanisms and escalate the crisis. Additionally, many of the individuals residing in this area are not newcomers. Many of the Arabs and others came during the Soviet invasion of Afghanistan. Unable to return to their own countries, they were forced to stay in this area. These individuals in many cases have married local women and have had children. Depending upon how long they have been settled, their children may have even attained the age when their betrothals may have been arranged.

This does not mean that the relationship between the native population and the foreign fighters who have moved in is free of friction. Far from it, there have always been tensions, related sometimes to tribal politics, and sometimes to the interaction between the tribes and the government of Pakistan.

Aside from the effects of tribal politics, there are a number of factors that influence the willingness (or lack thereof) to cooperate with the authorities. Of course, money and material play a vital role in getting cooperation from the tribesmen. However, any public display of such cooperation must have a moral legitimacy. For example, no matter how much money is offered, the tribesmen will not cooperate in the extradition of some people or groups whom they might deem weak and vulnerable, and they also view such efforts as bullying and against local norms. The same is true for Islam. No tribesmen in today's religious environment can risk being seen as working against the religion.

The utility of monetary buyouts to obtain tribal cooperation is speculative. For example, if a leader accepts money in exchange for cooperation, what happens to his authority, prestige, and honor? Presumably the answer depends on the particular conditions in which a tribal leader interacts. If a leader's taking of money is highly secretive and his tribesmen know little or nothing about it, then it will not be a problem for his prestige and public image. However, if he takes money for something that has little or no religious or moral defense, then taking money will be a problem and his tribe might not follow his decision.

Recent Developments

A development of particular salience was the agreements between the central government and tribal leaders and Taliban commanders based in North and South Waziristan, which have led to the withdrawal of government forces into their traditional forts. From the Pakistani standpoint, the deal is meant to separate the Taliban from al Qaeda and foreign fighters located in Waziristan, but it may represent a strategic decision on the part of Islamabad to support the reconstituted Taliban against the Karzai government in Afghanistan. In any event, the consequence of the agreements has been the de facto Talibanization of this region, which has been turned into a strategic operational base for attacks into Afghanistan.[9]

One of the interesting developments that came out of this arrangement was the fighting in March of this year between the Taliban faction in South Waziristan led by Maulvi Nazir, a former associate of Gulbuddin Hekmatyar, and Uzbeks from the Islamic Movement

---

8 Eliza Griswold, "Where the Taliban Roam," *Harper's Magazine*, September 2003.

9 See Tarique Niazi, "Pakistan's Peace Deal with Taliban Militants," Jamestown Foundation, *Terrorism Monitor*, Volume IV, Issue 19, October 5, 2006.

of Uzbekistan (IMU) based in South Waziristan. The Uzbeks reportedly lost some 200 of a total strength of about 1,000 in the fighting. The Pakistani government has presented the campaign against the IMU as evidence of the success of the peace deals it has reached with the Taliban, but it can also be seen as a conflict within the Ahmedzai—between the Yargulkhel section of the Zeli Khel, the largest of three clans into which the Ahmedzai are divided and which has provided sanctuary to foreign militants in Wana, and Nazir, who belongs to the smaller clan, the Kakakhel.

There are related questions that need to be answered: Why have only the Uzbeks been targeted and not other foreign fighters, particularly the Arabs who constitute the core of al Qaeda, or the Chechens? And why was Nazir, who belongs to a minor clan, able to prevail over the powerful Yargulkhel, who have produced several senior Taliban commanders? The answer may go back to the Pakistani government's agreements with the Taliban. As part of the deal, the Taliban has reportedly agreed to stop attacks against Pakistani interests, but the Uzbeks and their Ahmedzai supporters were more interested in jihad against the "hypocrites" (the Pakistani government) than against the "infidels" (the United States and its NATO allies in Afghanistan). It may have been this difference in priorities that divided the Uzbeks from the Taliban. The conclusion is that the parties interested in maintaining the arrangement between Islamabad and the Taliban decided to eliminate a troublesome player.[10]

The consequences of the Talibanization of Waziristan for counterterrorism in Afghanistan are obvious. Regardless of the progress that may be registered in operations against the Taliban in Afghanistan, if the Taliban is able to operate or support its operations from sanctuaries across the border, the prospects that the Afghan government and its allies could defeat the Taliban insurgency will greatly diminish. Therefore, a reversal of Pakistani policy vis-à-vis the Taliban and effective control of the border are critical to the success of the U.S. and NATO project in Afghanistan.

---

10 See Tarique Niazi, "The Taliban's Turf War in South Waziristan," Jamestown Foundation, *Terrorism Focus*, Volume IV, Issue 9, April 10, 2007; M. Ilyas Khan, "Pakistan's Tribals—Who Is Killing Who?" BBC News, April 5, 2007.

CHAPTER 7

Sad Wisdom of Hindsight: Soviet Intervention in Afghanistan (1979–1989)

Pavel K. Baev[1]

Introduction

The most fundamental lesson from the decade-long Soviet effort at building a governable satellite state from the rather unpromising available material could be concisely formulated as: If you think about invading Afghanistan, don't. We are obviously not learning this lesson—and that underpins the current search for other possibly relevant political and military lessons.

The differences between the two interventions at their start, respectively, on the Christmas day of 1979 and in late September 2001, are so vast that it would not be an overstatement to argue that the USSR invaded a different country. It certainly occupies the same place on the world map now as it did 25 years ago, but for the Soviet Union this was one of the easiest places to deploy a large grouping of forces, since Afghanistan was a neighbor country and the access to its northern part was wide open, while Central Asia provided a reliable rear base. The state that now is hugely traumatized by nearly 30 years of armed violence had been remarkably peaceful by the start of 1980s, when the warrior traditions existed only as legends.

It might be useful to note, however, that the geriatric Politburo had very limited information about the situation in Afghanistan outside the tiny group of 'revolutionaries' and relied on quite incomplete assessments of possible challenges.[2] The Bush administration, bustling with neo-con energy, to the contrary, had a clear picture of the potential theatre of operations and a reasonable general idea of what it was up to. The Soviet intervention, in short, was a blunder caused by profound misunderstanding of the internal crisis in Afghanistan, while the US intervention was a considered, justified, and necessary response to a direct attack of shocking viciousness.

While the Soviet occupation is typically perceived as a military enterprise, it was in fact a complex endeavor portrayed by Soviet propaganda in a slightly surrealistic way as performing an 'international duty', so some economic and political lessons might be uncovered in that slow-moving disaster as well. The relevance of these lessons, however, could be rather limited because the colossal increase of opium production, the massive societal changes under the impact of devastating wars, and the alliance between the endemic Taliban and the globalized Al Qaeda make the present-day security setting qualitatively different.

---

1 Pavel K. Baev is a research professor at the International Peace Research Institute (PRIO) in Oslo.

2 One thoughtful and informed analysis of Soviet decisionmaking on Afghanistan in the context of global geopolitical confrontation is Odd Arne Westad, *The Global Cold War* (Cambridge, UK: Cambridge University Press, 2005), particularly Chapter 8 on 'The Islamic Defiance: Iran and Afghanistan.' Of great value is also 'The Intervention in Afghanistan and the Fall of Détente,' Nobel Symposium 95, edited by David A. Welch and Odd Arne Westad (Oslo, 1996).

Economy Matters—But Does Not Work

Afghanistan has perplexed every European invader, perhaps since Alexander the Great, with the unanswerable question of how an economy so small could possibly support a population so large. The USSR had been providing economic assistance to Afghanistan for decades, but when it found itself in the position of 'owning' the country, that question still came up as a fundamental issue. The tentative answer was based on the model of Central Asian republics and included the controversial plan for land reform, which proved to be one of the key triggers of resistance; in the final analyses, that economic policy simply did not answer. Nevertheless, it is essential to acknowledge that much of the existing economic infrastructure, from roads and canals to power stations and grids, is Soviet-built and so its efficient maintenance requires cooperation with Russia.[3] It is possible, in principle, to replace every old power generator with a new US-designed 'made-in-China' model, but there probably are better ways to waste resources.

It is perhaps even more essential to reflect upon the fact that the last time that Afghanistan had a reasonably functioning (even if not exactly 'globalized' or 'market-liberalized') economy, it was significantly open to the North and connected to the economic structures of the USSR.[4] A proposition, if not a lesson, emerging from that observation is that without reconnecting the Afghan economy to the markets of Central Asia, corrupt as they are, and reestablishing economic links with Russia, whatever the commercial content, it is hard to expect any sustained economic revival.

One final observation on the economic factors is that the extreme poverty makes it all but impossible to deploy a grouping of armed forces that would be large enough for the purpose of forceful stabilization of Afghanistan, since the logistical problems become insurmountable.[5] The Russian 'limited contingent', which reached the maximum strength of 118,000 in 1985, lost 14,453 troops in the course of the war, while 53,753 soldiers were registered as wounded and 415,932 as seriously sick (hepatitis alone accounted for 115,308 cases). The quality of drinking water was the prime source of illness—and it has not improved since.

The Blunder of Geopolitics and the Priorities of 'Grand Strategy'

In both Moscow and Washington, the initial conceptualization of the rushed intervention into Afghanistan in autumn 2001 was shaped in no small measure by the inflated assessments of energy interests in the Caspian area that had earlier underpinned the mostly virtual 'Great Game' of the second half of the 1990s.[6] There is no need in revisiting here these spectacularly

---

[3] For a recent argument in favor of such proposition in the Russian media, see Aleksandr Kots, "Russia Returns to Afghanistan?" *Komsomolskaya Pravda*, April 20–26, 2007.

[4] See Barnett Rubin, "The Political Economy of War and Peace in Afghanistan," *World Development*, Vol. 28, No. 10, 2000, pp. 1789–1803.

[5] As Dominic Lieven pointed out, back in 1904, George Clarke, the Secretary to the Committee on Imperial Defence, called it 'sheer lunacy' to imagine that Russia could sustain large forces in Afghanistan: 'The great factors of war—supply and communication—are either ignored or absolutely miscalculated.' See Dominic Lieven, *Empire: The Russian Empire and Its Rivals*, New Haven, Conn.: Yale University Press, 2001, p. 109.

[6] One example is Ariel Cohen, ed., *Eurasia in Balance: The US and the Regional Power Shift*. Aldershot, UK: Ashgate, 2005.

false analytical constructs, but it may be useful to point out that is does not take a microscope to see the fact that the energy and counterterrorism policies have different geographic foci. Indeed, in US and European strategic thinking, the counterterrorism map is centered on Kabul and the Caspian energy map—on Baku; the distance between these two focal points is no less than 1,600 km. Russian military-security thinking is centered on Dushanbe and Bishkek, where Russian troops are based, while the energy-related assessments are concentrated about 1,000 km to the west, at the Caspian shores of Kazakhstan and Turkmenistan, where major oil and gas projects are being implemented. This wide gap inevitably brings a discrepancy between the presumably complementary efforts, while the persistent misperceptions generate mistrust and unnecessary competition between the United States and Russia.[7]

A peculiar parallelism with the situation in the early 1980s can be seen in this passage from a celebrated history work: '... a mood close to hysteria gripped the American public and private debate. How else (except, in part, by a staggering ignorance of Asian topography) are we to explain the American view, seriously put forward at the time, that the entry of Soviet troops into Afghanistan marked the first step of a Soviet advance that would soon reach the Indian Ocean and the Persian Gulf.'[8] The Soviet leadership was obsessed by their own geopolitical misperceptions, epitomized by Yury Andropov's point that '...we are dealing here with a struggle against American imperialism . . . for this reason we cannot retreat', and that prevented the military planners in the General Staff from seeing the troubles in Afghanistan for what they really were and dealing with them accordingly.[9]

Despite these geopolitical fantasies, Moscow remained remarkably sober about setting macro-strategic priorities. Afghanistan was certainly not the most important crisis that the USSR faced at the end of the decade of slow stagnation or Brezhnev's zastoi; the decision to intervene, however, indirectly but unmistakably determined several choices related to other crises. The decisions not to invade Poland—paralyzed with Solidarity strikes in 1980–1981—and to entrust the risky work of imposing martial law to Wojciech Jaruzelski were in many ways shaped by the burden of Afghanistan.[10] The consequences of Soviet control over Poland were positive in the short-term and disastrous in the mid-term; nevertheless, that restraint provided for the concentration of military efforts on one theatre, even if that massive deployment was still proven to be insufficient for victory. The parallel with the war in Iraq will not be drawn here, since it is obviously too late to contemplate this 'lesson'.[11] It appears interesting, however, to contrast that Soviet downplaying of the significance of the Afghan war with the present day

---

[7] I elaborated this argument in Pavel K. Baev, "Turning Counter-Terrorism into Counter-Revolution," *European Security*, Vol. 15, No. 1, March 2006, pp. 3–22.

[8] Eric Hobsbawm, *The Age of Extremes: A History of the World, 1914–1991,* New York: Vintage Books, 1994, p. 246.

[9] Politburo document of March 10, 1983, as cited in Andrew Bennett, *Condemned to Repetition?* Cambridge, Mass.: MIT Press, 1999, p. 238.

[10] Vojtech Mastny provided an insightful analysis of that crisis in "The Soviet Non-Invasion of Poland in 1980–1981 and the End of the Cold War," Woodrow Wilson Center, Cold War International History project, Working Paper no. 23, Washington, September 1998. For a relevant collection of documents, see Mark Kramer, "Soviet Deliberations During the Polish Crisis, 1980–1981," Special Working Paper no. 1, Woodrow Wilson Center, Washington, April 1999.

[11] Paul Krugman made a straightforward argument on 'arithmetic of insurgency' establishing that in Afghanistan 'we are trying to provide security to 30 million people with a force of only 32,000 Western troops and 77,000 Afghan national forces.' His bottom line was 'If we stop trying to do the impossible in Iraq, both we and the British would be able to put more troops in a place where they might still do some good.' See Paul Krugman, "The Math of Failure," *International Herald Tribune*, October 28–29, 2006.

NATO policy of portraying its operation as the ultimate test for the Alliance's cohesion and very viability, which in real terms is not necessarily the case. Overall, this over-selling of the complex peace-building/counterterrorist combat deployment as well as the spinning of 'Great Game' misperceptions translate into troubles for the prospects of regional cooperation.

The Empty Promise of Regionalism

The construction of the 'Friendship' bridge across the Amu-Darya River in 1982 did not signify an attempt by the USSR to engage Afghanistan in a cross-border cooperation, promising as that approach might have seemed. Indeed, fostering ties between the Turkmen, the Uzbek, and the Tajik SSR and the ethnically related communities on the other side of the border could have secured for the Soviet forces a reasonably safe rear area in Northern Afghanistan. The Soviet leadership, however, remained primarily concerned about the possibility of 'corrosive' influence from Afghanistan on the Muslim population of Central Asia, so the border remained tightly sealed. Mazari-Sharif was made into a reasonably secure 'entry point', but despite the propaganda work of 'advisers' from Tajikistan, the Tajik tribes in the Panjshir valley united by Akhmad Shah Masood fought against Soviet troops with utmost determination.

The proposition for re-launching regional cooperation and 'opening up' Afghanistan in the Northern direction in the framework of the Greater Central Asia Partnership for Cooperation and Development was advanced in 2004 by a couple of 'think-tanks' in Washington with a massive spin.[12] The argument in favor of a trade corridor from Gwadar on the Indian Ocean to Tashkent and Dushanbe appeared convincing indeed, but the initiative was derailed at the most inopportune moment by the massacre in Andijan, Uzbekistan, and the consequent disruption of the US-Uzbek relations, including the withdrawal from the K2 airbase.[13] The problem, however, runs deeper than just a particular disagreement; the emphasis in the coalition state-building efforts has been on democratization—and the ideas about competitive elections and power-sharing are distinctly alien for Messrs Karimov and Rakhmonov, as well as for Niyazov's successors. Stricken by fear of 'colored revolutions', they are inclined to see international NGOs as a far more immediate source of risk than the Taliban.

The northern borders of Afghanistan have therefore remained closed for most normal exchanges except, quite naturally, drug-trafficking. That has left the quite uncontrollable 'frontier' area of Northern Pakistan as the crucial interface for Afghanistan, which, on the one hand, leads to 'trans-nationalization' of internal crises in Pakistan, and, on the other, further increases the weight of the 'Pashtun factor' in Afghan politics.[14]

---

[12] One picture-perfect presentation is S. Frederick Starr, "A Partnership for Central Asia," *Foreign Affairs*, July–August 2005, pp. 164–178; see also Nicklas Norling, First Kabul Conference on Partnership, Trade and Development in Greater Central Asia, Washington, April 2006. For a different perspective, see Kristian Berg Harpviken, "Afghanistan: From Buffer State to Battleground—to Bridge Between Regions?" in James Hentz and Morten Bøås, eds, *Beyond the Nation State*, Aldershot, UK: Ashgate, 2003.

[13] One bitter reflection on that estrangement is John Daly et al., *Anatomy of a Crisis: US-Uzbekistan Relations, 2001–2005*, Washington: Silk Road Paper, February 2006.

[14] For an insightful discussion of this issue, see Kristian Berg Harpviken, "How Transnational Is the Taliban?" paper presented at the CSCW workshop, March 2007.

The Politics of the Non-Stop Civil War

Drawing parallels between present-day democracy-building in Afghanistan and Soviet efforts at steering it on the course of 'socialist orientation' might appear grossly politically incorrect besides being quite misleading. There is, nevertheless, a similarity between Babrak Karmal's total dependence upon the Soviet advisers and President Hamid Karzai's isolation behind the protective shield of US bodyguards. Both leaders are far more convincing to their international sponsors than they are to the domestic audience, and there may be a lesson in the fact that Moscow did eventually manage to find an alternative that was able to stand on his own feet; hence the surprising survivability of President Najibullah after the withdrawal of Soviet troops in early 1989.[15]

In fact, from the moment of the unexpected overthrow of the Daoud Khan's 'autocratic modernization' regime in April 1978, the Soviet leadership was struggling with the two interconnected tasks of expanding the support base of the 'vanguard party' and checking the violet squabbles inside that 'band of brothers'. The ideology of struggle against the 'class enemies' and Lenin's methodology of building a revolutionary party clashed with the practical needs of consolidating the regime, until Gorbachev hesitantly put the latter first. One conclusion that Moscow was slow to draw (since it did not fit into the Soviet model) was that Afghanistan could not be made into a centralized state run from a single consolidated seat of power. Authority and resources had to be shared on many levels and not simply distributed from Kabul, so that, in strategic terms, control over the capital was a necessary but by no means a sufficient precondition for success. To what degree that conclusion remains relevant today when the idea of federalism is greatly compromised by the experience with warlordism, is not a question beyond the limited competence of this author. It appears entirely possible that the preference for a strong 'security-provider' state expressed by many Afghans in 2002–2005 was an aberration, and the emergence on the political arena of the National Front, bringing together regional political forces (first of all the Tajiks and the Uzbeks) and the remnants of the Parcham and Khalq factions, might signal the beginning of a shift to 'normalcy'.[16]

Another conclusion, drawn to the contrary very early on (despite the sudden scare of the Herat mutiny in spring 1979), was that it was entirely possible to build a strong army and numerous police force (*tsarandoi*) that would remain reasonably loyal to the regime. That conclusion is not necessarily invalidated by the fact that the USSR was able to utilize the existing military structures, particularly the officer corps, while the United States and NATO have started building a new army from scratch. Two things, however, make a significant difference: (a) the Soviet Army did not have such a hard-driven and experienced adversary as the Taliban; and (b) the *tsarandoi* never faced the risk of mutating into a regional militia controlled by warlords deeply involved in heroin production.

---

[15] Hobsbawn (1994, p. 459), argued: 'The government of President Najibullah, to everyone's surprise, survived some years after the Soviet army left; and when it fell, it was not because Kabul could no longer resist the rural armies, but because a section of its own professional warriors decided to change sides.'

[16] This political development has attracted much attention in Moscow; see, for instance, Dmitri Verhoturov, "Another Afghanistan," Expert (Web site in Russian), 2007.

Strategy for Winning—or for Not Losing—War

The Soviet Army had had some tradition but no experience in 'unconventional' warfare by the start of the 1980s, or for that matter fighting experience of any kind, while its training remained predominantly focused on confronting NATO. The initial plan envisaged more a demonstration of force than a combat deployment, and the strategy of conducting the war was improvised along the way—and changed several times during the course of the war. The lessons, therefore, are quite contradictory—and there was never an attempt in the Russian General Staff at analyzing them in a systematic way.

Due to rigid ideological dogmas, it was quite impossible to formulate the goals of the war in any comprehensible way or to identify the enemy (except for the expressive term *dushman*) and analyze the driving forces of resistance other than US support. The pervasive propaganda cliché of 'performing an international duty' was in such shocking contrast with the reality on the ground that for the rank and file it was simply impossible to get a motivating answer to the blunt question 'What the hell are we doing here?'[17] The policy of 'big-brotherly' help and the strategy of 'deterrence by punishment' worked strictly cross-purpose, and the indiscriminate use of force was in fact a key factor in fuelling the resistance. More often than not, the brutal 'cleansing' of villages was the result of poor training of conscript units, but more generally, the rather high tolerance of Russian casualties went hand in hand with the even higher tolerance of 'collateral damage'. As the determination of mojahedeen resistance increased, more emphasis was placed on large-scale unconstrained application of air power, and while the current air strikes are far better targeted, every unintentional stray hit resonates strongly with the memories of devastating Russian bombardments.[18]

The deficit of clarity on the aims of war translated into the lack of answer on the key question about the course of hostilities: Is time on our side or not? The ideological interpretation of the conflict was unwaveringly optimistic—the 'backward' society was expected to recognize gradually the advantages of socialism and to learn to appreciate the charitable help of the USSR. That wishful thinking dictated a rather passive approach to operations (prevalent in 1981), since it was more important to win time than battles, while minimizing the burden was seen as an essential condition for sustaining the deployment. The pragmatic assessment of the situation by the General Staff, however, dictated a proactive strategy (adopted in 1982 and again in 1985), since only by defeating the elusive enemy in as many encounters as possible could the resistance be suppressed before it engulfed one province after another. No retrospective analysis can establish with any certainty whether the war had a 'military solution' or not, but it is quite clear that the USSR in its autumnal decade had neither the Stalinist determination nor the Leninist ingenuity to find one.[19]

Even at the peak of combat operations in 1985, the pursuit of this problematic 'military solution' was accompanied by negotiations on various levels, from the Geneva talks to dia-

[17] A typical reflection of this muddle was the traditional first Afghan toast: 'Za uspeh nashego beznadezhnogo dela' (For the success of our hopeless undertaking).

[18] An example that occurred exactly at the time of the conference was the airstrike on a madrasa in a remote corner of the Paktika province that killed seven children; see Barry Bearak and Taimoor Shah, "7 Children Killed in Airstrike in Afghanistan," *New York Times*, June 19, 2007.

[19] An interesting counterfactual case for achieving a 'pacification' of Afghanistan by provoking a new war between India and Pakistan is developed in David C. Isby, "Afghanistan: The Soviet Victory," in Peter G. Tsouras, ed., *Cold War Hot: Alternative Decisions of the Cold War*, London: Greenhill Books, 2003.

logues with particular warlords aimed at striking localized 'peace deals' without involving the Kabul government. The cease-fire in the Panjshir valley, agreed to with Akhmad Shah Masood in 1983, was significant in setting a precedent for such deals (even if the real aim was to prepare the spring offensive in 1984), and a number of similar accords provided for the relatively painless withdrawal of Soviet troops in 1988–1989. Najibullah continued this political bargaining until the warlords managed to strike a deal against him.[20] If there is a strategic lesson in that, it is probably about the talks that were not an alternative to fighting but rather a parallel track of political struggle; some useful results could be achieved but neither could trust be built nor a durable solution negotiated; the clear preference of the parties to any negotiations was to fight it out. An interesting insight into this pattern can be found in Joseph Brodsky's short poem 'On negotiations in Kabul', in which a meeting between Western ambassadors and 'cruel-hearted mountain tribes' is vividly described resulting in 'serpent signature on the agreement'—'and then there is nothing, none to see there, none at all. . . .'[21]

Tactics of Asymmetric Guerrilla War

Unlike the muddled strategy, the tactics of combat operations in Afghanistan were analyzed and evaluated by the Russian military establishment both during the war and after its inglorious end.[22] As the wars in Chechnya have shown, many of the lessons were neglected and unlearned—but that does not mean that they are entirely irrelevant. The 'enemy' in Afghanistan has not changed that much in the operational sense, so the Soviet experience in hitting and hammering on its weaknesses is worth a second look.

One counterintuitive feature of Soviet operations is the nearly complete absence of fighting in the cities or confronting any kind of urban guerrilla. The troops were garrisoned outside Kabul and the provincial capitals, and the tasks of policing and patrolling inside those cities were performed mostly by Afghan forces. Another feature that has to be kept in mind while looking into the encounters of various kinds is that the information revolution was a good decade away, so the Soviet Army did not have the advantages of GPS, modern communications, or real-time satellite intelligence.

The Soviet command learned quickly that regular Army units were not particularly useful assets, except for garrisoning key strategic points and for convoy duties, so the bulk of combat tasks was performed by tactical aviation and helicopters of the army aviation, as well as various mobile units, such as airborne brigades and reconnaissance battalions and, above all, Spetsnaz. These highly trained professional units were ideally suited for the rugged but open terrain with few roads but many trekking paths, so the Afghan campaign was the high point

---

20 Amin Saikal was scornful about that Machiavellian policy: 'Najibullah was prepared to compromise with literally any strongman inside or outside the country.' See Amin Saikal, *Modern Afghanistan: A History of Struggle and Survival*, New York: I. B. Tauris, 2004, p. 205.

21 My translation from Joseph Brodsky, 'K peregovoram v Kabule' (1992).

22 Detailed examination of many tactical episodes by the Frunze Military Academy can be found in Lester W. Grau, *The Bear Went Over the Mountain: Soviet Combat Tactics in Afghanistan*, London: Frank Cass, 1998 (the Russian original text is from 1991).

in the Spetsnaz history.[23] Many operations involved demonstrative movement of heavy armor towards a suspect village with Spetsnaz groups intercepting the retreating dushmans on their escape routes. On many other occasions these units were setting ambushes on caravan paths in order to cut supply to mojahideen strongholds in the mountains, thus engaging in guerrilla-type operations against a guerrilla adversary. The appearance of US Stinger shoulder-launched surface-to-air missiles in many mojahideen bands since 1986 increased the risks for the Mi-24 helicopter gunships that provided close air support in such operations.[24]

A major problem for most combat encounters was the shortage of tactical intelligence, since air reconnaissance had too many blind spots (there was no capacity for nighttime observation) and had to be supplemented with 'hum-int' from a variety of not particularly reliable sources. On many occasions, Spetsnaz and other units involved in ambushes, interdictions, and other special operations found themselves in carefully laid traps resulting in heavy casualties, particularly as the rescue helicopters were targeted on the ground. It was the lack of tactical intelligence that rendered the Soviet attempts at 'decapitating' the resistance by eliminating key mojahideen leaders so ineffectual, in contrast, for that matter, with the assassination of Akhmad Shah Masood by Al Qaeda on 9 September 2001 or with the more recent hit on Mullah Dadullah.[25]

Overall, Soviet tactics were moderately efficient in the middle phase of the war but were gradually countered with sufficient success and eventually defeated, not because of the delivery of Stingers and other military equipment from the United States but primarily as a result of accumulating combat experience in the mojahideen groups and expanding support for the resistance in the population. The limited application of 'scorched earth' tactics was strictly counterproductive in terms of deterring the guerrillas but undermined profoundly the positions of pro-Soviet political forces.

Conclusions

An observation of a knowledgeable US expert remains as true today as it was ten years ago: 'To this day the Western view of the Afghan War has been clouded by mystery and shadows.'[26] These shadows might even become darker as the spiral of violence continues to unfold, making Western efforts at simultaneously recreating a functional state and exterminating the networks of an Islamic quasi-state woefully inadequate. A closer look into these shadows would not necessarily be that informative, as dissimilarities become only more evident. The most striking difference is the present-day sharply lower threshold of pain coming from both taking and inflicting casualties; the wave of suicide bombings organized by the Taliban (a tactic that would have

---

23 A remarkable collection of firsthand accounts, particularly on the Afghan war, is S. Kozlov, ed., *Spetsnaz GRU-2: Voina ne okonchena, istoriya prodolzhaetsya* (Spetsnaz GRU-2: The war is not over, history continues), Moscow: Russkaya Panorama, 2002.

24 See Anthony Arnold, *The Fateful Pebble: Afghanistan's Role in the Fall of the Soviet Empire*, Novato, Calif.: Presidio Press, 1993, particularly pp. 138–139.

25 For a good profile, see Omid Marzban, "Mullah Dadullah: Military Mastermind of Taliban Insurgency," *Terrorism Focus*, March 21, 2006. See also "Taliban Names Slain Commander's Brother as Successor," *International Herald Tribune*, May 18, 2007.

26 David M. Glantz, "Introduction," in Grau, *The Bear Went Over the Mountain* (1998, p. xii).

hardly made much sense against the Soviet forces) exploits exactly this vulnerability. For that reason, this paper has never aimed at compiling a list of 'lessons', and instead offered a few suggestive rather than affirmative propositions.

The fundamental difference between the two operations is actually in the present-day twice-lower level of military engagement combined with the sharply higher price of defeat. For the Soviet leadership, it was certainly suboptimal, but still possible, to cut their losses out and seal off the border; for the Western coalition, there is no such option, and the return of the Taliban continues to be both looming and unthinkable. The Soviet experience proved convincingly that the deployment on the 100,000-level, sustained for many years, was not in itself a 'winning move'—and would not necessarily be now, even if such level of commitment were feasible. What appears both crucial and feasible is to invest in expanding and upgrading the Afghan army, for which the level of 100,000 should not be seen as the ceiling.

The final point in contemplating the past experience concerns engaging Russia more in state-building in Afghanistan, where it can make a significantly more constructive contribution than is currently the case. The concentration of cooperative effort in the Russia-NATO Council is perhaps unfortunate, not only because Moscow is growing increasingly suspicious to the alliance but also because its main contribution could be of economic and political character. The 'Great Game' paradigm should be scrapped and replaced by a 'Come Together' model.

CHAPTER EIGHT

The Next Afghanistan

Cheryl Benard[1]

Post-Taliban Afghanistan now looks back on almost six years of stabilization and nation-building operations. This is a suitable time to take stock, with two questions in mind: First, what lessons can we take away for the "next Afghanistan," and which course corrections suggest themselves for the "current Afghanistan"? In other words, what do we think were effective procedures to be replicated elsewhere; what do we consider to have been mistakes; and what should we learn from the latter?

Our conclusions can be summarized in five recommendations for future stabilization, post-conflict, and nation-building exercises:

- Get the best obtainable baseline before you "freeze" the conflict and begin with post-conflict operations.
- Question your analogies—the wrong analogy can distort your policies and lead to an incorrect approach.
- Keep sight of youth and women as sectors critical to the success of the mission, rather than viewing them as marginal groups included out of compassion.
- Take the concept of human security more seriously.
- Consider not just rocking the boat, but sinking the boat.

We will now consider these in turn.

Get the Best Obtainable Baseline

By baseline, in this context, we mean the situation prevailing on the ground at the moment when the conflict is declared to be ended and measures to prevent its resumption begin to be launched. It is natural—but incorrect—to assume that a conflict should be ended at the earliest possible opportunity. In fact, the point at which it is ended represents the point at which state-building and nation-building will have to begin. These are difficult enterprises and it is important to give them the optimal obtainable starting point.

In Afghanistan, the prevailing formula was almost exactly the opposite. The intervention was quick, brief, and had a very narrow goal: to eliminate the Taliban regime and make it impossible in the future for the country to be used as a safe haven by al Qaeda. Not only was

[1] Cheryl Benard is a senior political scientist with the RAND Corporation, where she also directs the Initiative for Middle Eastern Youth and the Alternative Strategies Series, focused on creating indigenous counter-levers to extremism and radicalization.

nation-building *not* taken into account, it was explicitly excluded as a goal of the American military intervention. This would change in relatively short order, but by the time it did, it was too late. Had a stable, democratic, modernizing Afghanistan been the goal from the outset, a number of important things would presumably have been done differently. The Northern Alliance and its collection of historically freighted warlords would presumably not have been allowed to—essentially—"conquer" the country on behalf of the United States. One would probably have planned for economic development and for a longer and larger international presence from the start.

Question Your Analogies

The approach decided on for Afghanistan rested on a number of assumptions, many of which were drawn from a certain way of reading Afghan history and culture. Thus, it was decided to keep a low profile and to maintain a "small footprint." Proxies—Northern Alliance troops—were used in place of a U.S. invading ground force, on the assumption that a foreign presence would rile the Afghans. Table 8.1 shows an overview of the policy approaches that were decided upon before, during, and immediately after the overthrow of the Taliban, as well as the reasoning behind these decisions. It is our contention that all of these decisions were wrong and that each rested on an incorrect assumption.

The operating assumptions were drawn from a variety of sources. These included a deep-seated stereotypical image of Afghanistan as a remote, distant, archaic, and quaint society. They rested on conclusions drawn from colonial history and from the Soviet experience in Afghanistan. In discussions of Afghanistan, there was a pronounced tendency to slip into a sort of generalized "lay anthropologist" mode. Meetings were rife with observations about Pashtuns, tribal societies, the Afghan national character, and the like. These clichés were so overpowering that the emerging civil society within that population, as well as the changes that had occurred during three decades of conflict, were not taken into account.

In retrospect, it is clear that the assumptions were incorrect in some important regards. During the first years following the overthrow of the Taliban, Afghans in general wanted a larger, not a smaller, international and ISAF presence. International forces were thought to be more neutral, not to be corrupt, and not to have the exploitative agenda of local police or of the warlord militias.

A policy of minimal goals and minimal intervention meant letting the warlords and druglords continue to thrive. The hope was that, if they were integrated into the newly emerging structures, they would see a role and a place for themselves and would cooperate, and thus would not have to be taken on militarily, which the Coalition was not prepared to do. The underlying calculation was that participation in a modern democratic system would transform them, at least over time. They would increasingly be obliged to play by the new rules. Their feudal support base would erode as their militias were disarmed and their supporters drifted into the new institutions of a national police and army.

While this may still occur, things do not look encouraging. The narco-drug trade is, by all accounts, out of control, and the presence of despised individuals with atrocious human rights records has undermined popular support for the Karzai government, which is seen as either uncaring or as too weak to do anything about the matter.

Table 8.1
Underlying Assumptions Versus the Actual Situation in Afghanistan

Approach	Underlying Assumption	Actual Situation
Small footprint[a]	Afghans historically resent and resist any foreign presence	After years of civil war and Taliban misrule, Afghans trusted foreigners more than they trusted domestic authorities. They actually desired a larger, not a smaller presence, at least during the first years.
Low goals: sufficient if country was no longer an al Qaeda base of operations[b]	Very backward, traditional country of low strategic importance except as a safe haven to terrorists	Afghanistan was ripe for dramatic change, with the majority of the population on board for development and reform. Its location was actually of preeminent strategic importance.
Don't attempt much social reform, especially in regard to gender, tribal structures, and Pashtun customs[c]	Doing so caused the Soviets to fail, as Afghanistan is a highly conservative society and there is no real support base for modernity, democracy, or reform.	Afghanistan had changed since the Soviet invasion. The population was by and large now open to elections, schooling (including girls' schools), and employment for women. They were tired of corruption and the arbitrary rule of warlords.
Don't rock the boat—bring important stakeholders, including warlords and druglords, into the system instead of attempting to eliminate them.[d]	Being extremely backward, Afghanistan can only democratize and develop slowly. Over much time, that process of development will crowd out the feudal, tribal structures. Taking these structures on directly would require a higher effort level, investment, and presence than desired.	A dangerous gamble, resting on several daring assumptions: that a fragile democratization process would win out over the centuries-old stranglehold of tribal and traditional elites; that the elites would not understand or would not resist this slow, half-hearted attempt at their attrition; that it would not be even more expensive if this approach failed and the Taliban and/or al Qaeda reestablished themselves in the neighborhood.

[a] The light footprint approach is attributed to Lakhdar Brahimi, who served as the special administrator of the United nations Mission to Afghanistan. For more information, see Lakhdar Brahimi, *Shaping a Constitution: The UN's "Light Footprint" Approach in Afghanistan*, United Nations Association of America, December 2004; Scott McMahon, "UN: 'Light Footprint' in Afghanistan Could Hold Lessons for Iraq," *Radio Liberty/Radio Free Europe*, April 2003.

[b] This fact is illustrated by the U.S. military leadership's ideological and resources-based support for warlords, mobilizing them to fight against al Qaeda operatives with little attention to the negative consequences. See Thomas Carothers, "Promoting Democracy and Fighting Terror," *Foreign Affairs*, January–February 2003.

[c] Many U.S. policymakers see violence as an endemic and irretractable "culture" in Afghanistan; for more information, see Sam Zia-Zarifi, *Losing the Peace in Afghanistan*, Human Rights Watch, World Report, 2004; Antonio Donini, *Nation Building Unraveled: Aid Peace and Justice in Afghanistan*, Bloomfield, Conn,: Kumarian Press, Inc., 2004.

[d] For example, Ambassador Swanee Hunt writes of an exchange with a Pentagon official in 2003: "When I urged him to broaden his search for the future leaders of Iraq, which had yielded hundreds of men and only seven women, he responded, 'Ambassador Hunt, we'll address women's issues after we get the place secure'" (Swanee Hunt, "Let Women Rule," *Foreign Affairs*, May–June 2007; Cheryl Benard et al., *Women and Nation Building*, Santa Monica, Calif.: RAND Corporation, MG-579-CMEPP, 2008).

Stereotypical views of Afghanistan prevented international policymakers from noticing that social development and rule of law had come to be valued by the Afghan mainstream, and that Afghanistan in the year 2001/2002 was not the same country it had been in the 1800s or even the 1900s.

Keep Sight of Youth and Women as Critical Sectors

The minimalist, small-footprint, "don't rock the boat" approach has especially significant consequences for minorities, women, and youths. In traditional, hierarchical societies operating on a logic of entitlement and vested interests, their rights and opportunities tend to be strongly constrained. Once the gears in Afghanistan had shifted and nation-building became the official goal, women were built into the effort.[2] Mindful of the supposed lessons of the failed Soviet experience, the inclusion of women was approached cautiously. However, Afghan society proved unexpectedly receptive to advances in gender issues. Women's large-scale participation in the political process, as voters and as candidates, aroused little resistance. However, the international community's efforts in this regard have been uneven. The most significant exclusion is in the area of law, where tribal traditions and non-Islamic customs have been allowed to continue unchallenged, even where they stand in crass contradiction to human rights, shariat law, and secular Afghan law.

Research shows that hierarchical societies (those in which ethnicity, class, and gender form the basis of stratified social orders) are more likely to use violence to resolve political disputes with neighboring states and are less stable domestically. Therefore, while it may be difficult, establishing a social order based on equality is also the best guarantor of creating a state that will maintain peaceful relations with its neighbors and will not experience civil war.

Instead of a cautious, piecemeal approach, the data argue for the early, energetic inclusion of women in a reconstruction and stabilization effort. A broad range of studies supports that recommendation. Women's economic participation is crucial, because women's income is more likely to be invested in health, education, and family well-being, thus encouraging development. With corruption representing a preeminent challenge to the establishment of healthy institutions, women's equitable presence in the police and in government bureaucracies has been found to decrease corruption levels.[3] In terms of stabilization operations, military commanders report receiving operational information for counterterrorist operations from female beneficiaries of PRT-delivered health and other civilian aid programs. To consider the social advancement of women a "luxury item" that should be placed on the agenda only when the situation is calm, is to misread the facts. Rather, increasing equity also increases the likelihood that a society will be peaceful and stable. As a World Bank study reported, "Gender equality is . . . a matter of international security in predicting state aggressiveness internationally."[4]

More than the interests of women, the interests of youths were marginalized in the Afghan reconstruction effort. While in the case of women, an overly energetic effort to elevate their status was thought to be risky, potentially destabilizing an already rocky enterprise, youths are ignored for different reasons. First, they have no forceful lobby, and second, education is viewed as their preeminent issue.

---

[2] See Cheryl Benard et al., *Women and Nation-Building*, Santa Monica, Calif.: RAND Corporation, MG-579-CMEPP, 2008.

[3] Cheryl Benard, Kristen Cordell, and Olga Oliker, *Women and Human Security: The Case of Post-Conflict Afghanistan*, WIIS Words, Women in International Security, Georgetown University Press, Summer 2007.

[4] Elizabeth King and Andrew Mason, *Engendering Development Through Gender Equality in Rights, Resources, and Voice*, Volume 1, A World Bank Policy Report, 2001; also see Isobel Coleman, "The Payoff from Women's Rights," *Foreign Affairs*, Vol. 83, No. 3, June 2004, pp. 80–95; Mary Caprioli, "Gender Equality and State Aggression: The Impact of Domestic Gender Equality on State First Use of Force," *International Interactions*, No. 29, 2003, pp. 195–214.

Perhaps because women have a strong advocacy movement while youths do not, awareness of the need to build policies adequate to the needs of youths is even less developed than policies geared to gender. A host of legal, economic, social, and planning needs surround the youth issue, but in implementation, the youth topic is often reduced to issues of schools and education. This is a serious oversight. Failure to integrate youths into the nation-building effort may have partially contributed to the resurgent Taliban, which acts as a magnet for disaffected, unemployed young men.

For many reasons—because of their sheer demographic significance, for one, and because their assets and attitudes will determine the future course of their societies—youths need to be a principal focus area, not an afterthought, of nation-building. Metrics based on the number of schools re-opened are irrelevant at best. The nature of those schools, of their curriculum, and of the resources their graduates will possess are far more important. In a post-conflict environment, equipping young people with practical life skills, inculcating new values through civic education, and readying them for gainful economic activity are essential. This should be supplemented with constructive leisure activities. In terms of human capital, young people and women are where the emphasis needs to lie. Both groups are critical as disseminators of new attitudes and of knowledge and information. Given their role in the family, women are crucial conduits of information and knowledge about basic health; they are also a potential instrument of socialization, able to spread new values to their children. Young people, more open to new methods and ideas, can similarly serve as conduits of health and other information from the schoolroom into their families. Most importantly, persuading the young that the new nation can work, and that they can have a positive and desirable life in this new system, is an absolute precondition for the prevention of new outbreaks of violence. The old order and its conflicts can only be deprived of ready recruits if the young see a better alternative.

Take the Concept of Human Security Seriously

The concept of human security has gained in currency in the previous years, but it has yet to anchor itself sufficiently in the actual approaches and policies of nation-building. Human security is defined broadly as a composite of conditions that together enable the average person in a society to live a life of reasonable safety from threats of violence, poverty, and disease. This includes feeling free from routine intimidation and from excessive levels of crime; having a reasonable level of overall hygiene and not facing extreme threats to physical survival due to public health hazards or poverty. Where human security is present, the individual has a reasonable opportunity to experience a reasonably good quality of life in relative freedom and safety from external threats. This has been found to best capture the desires and aspirations of ordinary populations globally. It is of little use to a normal person if the war has ended, but armed gangs are patrolling the neighborhood, free to terrorize the population. Human security is a concept designed to reflect what is actually required, in the real world, for a human being to feel secure in his or her life. This should be the overarching standard by which programs and policies are measured.

In Afghanistan, the international community of planners fell short in this regard. It took two years for health and hygiene—which were in an abominable state in Afghanistan and caused extremely high infant, child, and maternal mortality rates—to even be identified as priorities.

Meanwhile, the decision to co-opt rather than confront the stakeholders kept warlords and druglords in the game.[5] This in turn contributed to the reestablishment of a system based on nepotism, patronage, and corruption rather than on merit or rule of law. In a number of instances, egregious abuses were tolerated, eroding the public hope that a government operating on principles of law and justice was in the process of being installed. For example, the known killer of the Doctors Without Borders workers was briefly arrested, then allowed to go free due to his relationship with a powerful local leader.

Consider Not Just Rocking the Boat, But Sinking the Boat

The U.S. premise, as we set out to eliminate the Taliban regime, can be summarized in the following few sentences:

> Afghanistan needs to be brought into the fold of the international community because, as a rogue state, it harbors terrorists who represent a clear and present danger. For this, the Taliban regime needs to be overthrown. However, if we are too visible a presence, the Afghans will rise up against us because they do not tolerate foreign occupiers. Therefore, it is better to operate through the Northern Alliance, problematic though many of its leaders are on human rights and political grounds. Once the Taliban has been eliminated, a new government composed of the most important former stakeholders should be cobbled together. This is the formula most likely to guarantee stability.

Gradually, the assessment changed and the goals became more ambitious. The loya jirgas, the drafting of the constitution, and the elections all went well. The country seemed more receptive than initially anticipated to the notion of change, progress, and Western help. At the same time, the country was far more backward, its capacity to absorb and manage resources far more constrained, than had been expected. This necessitated a growing on-the-ground presence to make things function.

Six years into the effort, fault lines are appearing. The population is beginning to balk at repeated instances of "collateral damage," civilian casualties from badly targeted air strikes. The drug trade is eluding all efforts to control it. Neglect of human security goals is leading the population to become disenchanted with its government. In retrospect, a bolder and more costly approach early on might have been more economical in the end, if it had succeeded in eliminating the problems that have not only lingered but have grown, and if it had put a more healthy and solid foundation in place.

Course Correction?

Corrective action in Afghanistan today would probably need to consist of a multipronged effort to bolster the democratization effort. A strong and concerted emphasis on youths should

[5] This fact is illustrated by the U.S. military leadership's ideological and resources-based support for warlords, mobilizing them to fight against al Qaeda operatives with little attention to the negative consequences. See Thomas Carothers, "Promoting Democracy and Fighting Terror," *Foreign Affairs*, January–February 2003.

be the cornerstone of such a change. They should be the beneficiaries of an energetic civic education, vocational training, and economic orientation program.

Visible, exemplary action in matters of anticorruption and rule of law will also need to be taken. The druglords and warlords have not just "withered away"—herefore, they will need to be taken out in direct confrontation.

The above steps will be more difficult now than they would have been at the outset. By many reports, the mainstream population is losing faith and confidence in the national government. Bad players have become wealthier and more entrenched. And the international community is tiring of the issue. At the same time, civil society has made strides, the country is today far more connected to the global community, and important infrastructure improvements have been made. There is still time to take corrective action.

CHAPTER 9

Are We Learning? Military Engagement: The Taliban, Past and Present

Samina Ahmed[1]

To assess the directions of the insurgency in Afghanistan, and to adopt effective counterinsurgency strategies, it is essential not just to understand the role of the Taliban in driving the insurgency but also to learn lessons from the Taliban's past. It is equally important to discount and demolish myths about the Taliban if ongoing efforts to stabilize Afghanistan are to succeed.

A reinvigorated Taliban are undermining attempts to extend Kabul's authority over insurgency-hit regions, particularly in southeastern Afghanistan. The insurgency is also undermining the international community's efforts to help rebuild the infrastructure and institutions of the war-torn state. Absent security in the south and east, the rest of the country, now relatively peaceful, could slide back into internal conflict. As the insurgency rages, DDR (disarmament, demobilization, and reintegration) of armed factions has come to a virtual halt since powerholders in the north, west, and centre are unwilling to give up their guns in the light of the Taliban threat.

Warlords and commanders in southern and eastern Afghanistan are hedging their bets, and will likely make their decision based on their assessment of the international community's role. Ordinary citizens are in no position to confront the heavily armed insurgents. Fearing that the high costs of the conflict would weaken the international resolve to retain forces in Afghanistan, local stakeholders are unwilling to oppose the Taliban, since the price, as in the past, could be exorbitant. The international community's continued and robust military, political, diplomatic, and economic support could, however, dispel these fears, providing the time and space needed to ensure that the Afghanistan experiment is taken to its logical conclusion—a democratic state with stable institutions that serve the people, which would undermine the capacity of spoilers to derail the process.

Learning from the Past

Yet even today, as in the past, some influential external actors, particularly Pakistan, are attempting to depict the Taliban as credible and legitimate local stakeholders who, if included in the process, would only help stabilize Afghanistan's Pashtun belt. This myth is based on another—

[1] Samina Ahmed is Project Director for South Asia at the International Crisis Group. She worked previously as a research fellow at the Belfer Center for Science and International Affairs at the John F. Kennedy School of Government, Harvard University.

that the Taliban emerged as a Pashtun religious force in the 1980s in a spontaneous reaction to the excesses of warlords and subsequently rid their region of predators, gaining control over most of Afghanistan with little resistance since they had overwhelming local support.

The Taliban were indeed Pashtun, but they were not local religious leaders, heading a grassroots movement to rid their country of rapacious commanders and warlords. Mullah Omar and many of his closest allies were mujahideen commanders who had played an active part in the U.S.-led anti-Soviet jihad. As such, the Taliban were yet another mujahideen faction. Omar, for instance, was a supporter of Maulvi Younis Khalis' Hizbe Islami. Mullah Hasan Rehmani, Taliban Governor of Kandahar, had been with Maulvi Nabi Mohammedi's Harakat-e-Inquilab Islami; Jalaluddin Haqqani, who joined the Taliban in 1995, was a mujahideen commander from Paktia province.[2]

While the core of the Taliban leadership was composed of mujahideen commanders, their recruits were Afghan refugees as well as Afghan and Pakistani Pashtun Talibs (*Talibs* or *Taliban* is the plural for student), educated in madrasas in Balochistan and Northwest Frontier (NWFP), run by Pakistan's largest Islamist party, the Deobandi Jamiat Ulema-e-Islam (JUI) Province. And just as the mujahideen had a very secular, political goal in mind—to capture state power—so too the Taliban goal was to oust rival factions, ethnic and political, with the ultimate goal of controlling the state.

The Taliban managed to rapidly capture territory in Afghanistan for two reasons. First and foremost, the Pashtun force benefited from Pakistani assistance—political, diplomatic, and economic. The Taliban were allowed to use Pakistani territory as sanctuary and a base for recruitment, with the Pakistan army also providing arms, training, logistical support, and military assistance.[3] Second, the Taliban's initial success in eliminating rivals in southeastern Afghanistan convinced other Pashtun commanders to join the winning side. This process of co-optation was primarily based on the conviction that the Taliban would soon rule Afghanistan.

Their domestic and regional apologists and supporters claim that the Taliban's success was based on their ability to provide security and establish law and order, which in Afghanistan's war-torn environment required brute force. It is also argued that the Taliban's version of radical Sunni Deobandi Islam, superimposed on Pashtunwali, the Pashtun tribal code, was, after all, a part of Afghan culture.

Locals in southeastern Afghans might indeed have initially welcomed the Taliban because even a degree of security was preferable to the tyrannical and anarchical control of predatory warlords. Yet the Taliban's "disregard for local leaders and local processes"[4] soon alienated many, as did their implementation of an ultra-orthodox interpretation of the Islamic Sharia, superimposed on Pashtunwali.

Indeed, the Taliban interpretation of Islam and its political application was not rooted in Afghan culture. Eighty percent of Afghans follow the liberal Sunni Hanafi sect; Islam of the Sufi orders has popular support throughout Afghanistan. "Before the Taliban, Islamic

---

2 Rashid, Ahmed, *Taliban: The Story of the Afghan Warlords*, London: Pan Books, 2000, pp. 17–19, 22.

3 Anthony Davis, "How the Taliban Became a Military Force," in William Malley, ed., *Afghanistan and the Taliban: The Rebirth of Fundamentalism*, New York: Vanguard, 2001, pp. 69–70. See also "The Taliban File," Part 111, The National Security Archive, March 19, 2004.

4 Chris Johnson and Jolyon Leslie, *Afghanistan: The Mirage of Peace*, New York: Zed Books, 2004, p. 49.

extremism had never flourished in Afghanistan."[5] The Taliban leadership and commanders were influenced by JUI's Deobandi philosophy, and many were the graduates of the JUI's madrasas. Moreover, while the Taliban were Pashtuns, all Pashtuns were not Talibs. Pashtuns in Afghanistan were and remain deeply divided along clan, tribal, and regional lines. Then, as now, the acceptance of the Taliban's political and military dominance in Afghanistan's Pashtun belt was based far less on willing acceptance than on fear of retribution or a pragmatic willingness to support the winning side.

If this was the case within the Pashtun belt, non-Pashtuns had even more to fear, and with good reason. Ethnic reprisals and the imposition of an alien culture on the Hazaras, Tajiks, and Uzbeks reinforced the ethnic and regional hostilities that had fuelled the civil war. However, with Pakistan's military backing, the Taliban managed to impose their control over 90 percent of territory by 2001, with their rival Northern Alliance, representing the smaller ethnic groups, only holding a small sliver of territory in the north. Yet the Taliban failed, despite measures such as curbs on poppy production, to gain international recognition for their regime, not because of the brutality of their rule, but because of their unwillingness to part the ways with Osama bin Laden and his al Qaeda.

Post-Taliban Afghanistan

It is debatable whether the Taliban would have, absent international dynamics post 9/11, managed to consolidate their control. By 2001, aside from "growing signs of splits and dissents within the Taliban leadership", the "tribal Pashtuns demonstrated growing resentment against the strictures and corruption of Taliban rule and their lack of consideration for the suffering population", even in Kandahar, their heartland.[6] Local opposition to Taliban control grew not only because of the Taliban's brutal rule but also due to their failure to provide the economic goods. Even absent international intervention, this upsurge of opposition would have at the very least posed serious challenges to regime consolidation.[7]

When the Taliban were ousted from their last base, Kandahar, in December 2001, their departure was welcomed not just by the Hazaras, Uzbeks, and Tajiks but also in Pashtun-majority southern and eastern Afghanistan. There was little resistance to the international intervention countrywide. While the Taliban's ethnic and military rivals supported the international intervention, many co-opted commanders chose, once again, to join the winning side. Given the lack of domestic ownership, the Taliban's politico-religious order also fast collapsed.

Yet only six years after their ouster, the Taliban have re-emerged reinvigorated, leading an insurgency that is destabilising the southern Pashtun heartlands and making its presence felt in the eastern provinces. In the past weeks and months, insurgent attacks, including suicide bombings, have taken place countrywide, even in the provinces that border Kabul and also in the hitherto peaceful west and north.

---

5 Rashid (2000, p. 85).

6 Rashid (2000, p. 79).

7 Ali Jalali and Lester W. Grau, "Whither the Taliban?" *The Cyber-Caravan*, March 6, 1999.

The Resurgent Taliban

The media tends to attribute the insurgency solely to the Taliban, who are depicted as the prime perpetrators of violence. While Taliban commanders are driving the violence, many from Pakistani sanctuaries, only 20 percent of insurgents are ideological "Taliban."[8] They are backed by nonideological recruits and allies, including those who oppose Kabul, local leaders, or the international presence for their own reasons, but who have chosen to do so under the Taliban banner.

There are fluid alliances of convenience at the local level, albeit with little coherence or cohesion among different groups. Former foes of the Taliban, such as Gulbuddin Hekmatyar, have joined hands with them, motivated by the desire to prevent Kabul from extending its control and the state's nascent democratic institutions from stabilising. The alliance also includes old allies, such as al Qaeda, as well as spoilers, such as local warlords or drug traffickers. These spoilers are not only seeking to retain or gain access to power; for them the conflict is also "an economically profitable state of affairs, providing an environment in which they could pillage the country's resources or deal in illegal goods".[9] The drugs trade thus becomes a symptom and a cause of the insurgency. The Taliban and their allies profit from the drugs trade, and the drugs trade in turn at least partially finances the insurgency.

The Taliban's command and control structure has been constantly adapted to thwart counterinsurgency operations. After the Taliban ouster, some leaders revived their operational base within Afghanistan, conducting operations out of eastern and southern Afghanistan. Others, who had taken refuge in Pakistan, were to establish command and control structures in Balochistan, the Federally Administered Tribal Areas (FATA), and NWFP. A number of top Taliban commanders have been killed, including Mullah Akhtar Mohammad Osmani in December 2006 and Mullah Dadullah Akhund (the operational commander in four provinces in southwestern and central Afghanistan) in May 2007.[10] Because of their loose command and control structures in Afghanistan and Pakistan, the Taliban have, however, been able to absorb these losses.

Mullah Omar had run the Taliban-controlled state through a shura (council) of high-ranking Taliban leaders and commanders. In the wake of the Taliban's ouster, he reportedly set up a shura of hard-line Taliban commanders (the Rahbari Shura or Leadership Council) in 2003. The Quetta shura oversees fighting in the former Taliban heartlands of Kandahar, Uruzgan, and Helmand. There are other leadership bases within Afghanistan and in Pakistan's tribal belt, for instance, in South and North Waziristan. Hekmatyar's Hizb-e-Islami operates in Nuristan and Kunar, reaching as far inland as Laghman, Ghazni, and Logar, and in parts of the North. Jalaluddin Haqqani, the former Hizbe Islami commander who had joined the Taliban in 1995, has his own network, including madrasas, which are largely independent and self-sustaining. His influence, and his son Sirajuddin's, is prominent in southeastern Afghanistan, through areas of Ghazni.

Parts of FATA are now virtually under the control of the Taliban's Pakistani allies because of ill-advised peace deals between General Musharraf's military and Pakistani pro-Taliban

---

[8] International Crisis Group, *Countering Afghanistan's Insurgency: No Quick Fixes*, Report No. 123, November 2, 2006, p. 8.

[9] Johnson and Leslie (2004, p. 15).

[10] The Taliban Shura appointed Mullah Bakht Mohammad, Dadullah's younger brother, as his successor.

militants. As a result, the Taliban and their local allies have been ceded a secure base of operations. The end result is the enormous increase in cross-border attacks on Kabul's security forces and the international military, threatening to turn eastern Afghanistan, as in the case of the south, into an area where the Taliban can operate freely.[11]

In the early days of the insurgency, the Taliban benefited from ill-advised international policies. The light footprint was largely to blame, as was the US initial reluctance to see an international security presence outside Kabul, which could hinder US counterterrorism operations. Instead of a robust international security presence and an extension of the NATO–International Security Assistance Force (ISAF) mandate, the United States co-opted some of the most undesirable of mujahideen commanders to advance counterterrorism goals in southern and eastern Afghanistan. Exploiting this security vacuum in the south, the Taliban managed to regroup and reorganise. By the time ISAF's reach was extended, the international forces faced a well-armed and organised opposition.

Civilian casualties, commanders conducting local vendettas with international acquiescence, and the absence of the peace dividend have collectively created a fertile environment that the insurgents are exploiting. As a result of the insurgency, development has also ground to a halt in the south, fuelling local alienation. Moreover, the Karzai government's failure to deliver good governance, opting instead for shortcuts, including alliances of convenience with undesirable local allies, has provided the insurgents an opportunity to undermine its legitimacy. Given the resurgent insurgency and the lack of security, combined with fear of retribution, many locals are unsurprisingly reluctant to confront the Taliban. Others, particularly local commanders, could join the Taliban if they perceive that they are militarily ascendant. Growing local concerns that the international community intends to reduce its military presence in Afghanistan and could even withdraw before the state is stabilised fuel this perception.

Following the international intervention, there were high expectations for the peace dividend and widespread support for the new state-building enterprise. Despite Taliban threats, for instance, Pashtuns participated, albeit in smaller numbers than elsewhere, in the presidential and parliamentary elections. Had a decision been taken then to expand the international security presence to the south and east, and had Kabul opted for good governance instead of co-opting predatory warlords into local structures of governance and security, the insurgents could not have gained ground easily. Had there also been an international recognition then, as is gradually growing now, that the insurgency cannot be effectively tackled without dealing with the cross-border aspects, the threat it now poses could have been minimized. Relative security would also have allowed development to proceed apace, further reducing local support or acceptance of the Taliban.

Neglecting the Pakistani role was therefore a crucial error, and one that will have to be urgently addressed if the international community is to successfully stabilise the state. To prevent Afghanistan from once again descending into chaos and becoming a haven for criminals and terrorists, the international community must work collectively in addressing this challenge.

In end-2001, key Taliban commanders and thousands of supporters, along with their al Qaeda allies, fled to Pakistan. The Taliban now have sanctuaries in Pakistan. Their command and control centres are based in Pakistan's bordering provinces of Balochistan, Northwest

---

11 See International Crisis Group, *Pakistan's Tribal Areas: Appeasing the Militants*, Report No. 125, December 11, 2006.

Frontier Province, and the adjoining FATA region. There is an endless flow of recruits from Afghan refugee camps as well as Afghan and Pakistan Pashtuns from Deobandi madrasas.[12] Command and control centres, and access to arms, training, and finances in Pakistan, as well as support by Musharraf's Islamist allies, particularly the JUI-F that dominates the Balochistan and NWFP provincial governments, are feeding the Afghan insurgency, which now threatens to spread far beyond the Taliban's traditional heartland to encompass many regions that were hitherto stable.

Countering the Insurgency

The vast majority of Afghans do not want a return of Taliban-style governance. Nor have they lost all faith in the international community's ability to deliver security and the benefits of peace. Moreover, most Afghans still see the international military presence as the only guarantor of stability, which would prevent the state from sliding back into all-out civil war. However, in the worst insurgency-hit areas, such as southern Afghanistan, disillusionment with the international community is certainly increasing. Caught in the crossfire between the insurgents and the international forces, people have yet to see their lives improve. While the Taliban are responsible for the unstable environment that has hindered development, masters of propaganda, they are attempting, and with a certain amount of success, to woo disillusioned locals to their side.

As the insurgency spreads, the Taliban's factional and ethnic rivals are unwilling to give up their arms, bringing the disarmament process to a virtual halt. Even powerful factions within government, particularly in the security ministries, are unwilling to disband their militias and to disarm. In Afghanistan today, with the army and police still too weak to effectively assert Kabul's control, the international military presence plays a vital role in upholding the peace and stabilising the state.

Since development and expanding the reach of the state are also contingent on security, that international military presence must be maintained and strengthened, but minus country caveats. Troop-contributing states must be persuaded to be more flexible and remove restrictions that impede true interoperability of the international forces. The attacks in Afghanistan's west and north show that no part of the country is safe until and unless the insurgency is effectively countered.

At the same time, the international community must pressure Pakistan to take effective action against the Taliban, detaining Taliban leaders and closing down command and control centres. The flow of funds and arms to the Taliban must end, as should recruitment in Pakistani territory. The Pakistan government must also extend its writ over the tribal belt, particularly in FATA, which has, for all practical purposes, become a mini-Taliban state, largely due the military's policy of appeasing pro-Taliban local militants.[13]

Countering the insurgency in Afghanistan will also depend on internal reform. Until and unless Kabul cleans up its act, the Taliban shall continue to exploit Kabul's fast-eroding credibility. Poor governance, rampant official corruption, a predatory police, and the reliance of the

[12] Zahid Hussain, *Frontline Pakistan: The Struggle with Militant Islam*, New York: Columbia University Press, 2007, pp. 86–87.

[13] International Crisis Group, *Pakistan's Tribal Areas* (2006).

centre on discredited powerbrokers have eroded Kabul's standing. To win back the trust of the Afghan people, the Karzai government must end the culture of impunity. With international assistance, it must tackle judicial and police reform in earnest and concentrate on delivering the public good.[14]

Finally, if the insurgency is to be effectively tackled, Kabul and its international allies must not fall into the trap of appeasing the Taliban. Since 2006, with the insurgency gaining ground in southeastern Afghanistan, Kabul and some of its international supporters have begun to debate the desirability as well as the mechanisms of bringing the Taliban back into the political fold.[15] Pakistan is also pushing for an inclusion of the Taliban in government.

The Afghan parliament has called for reconciliation and recommended a general amnesty with all warring factions, including the Taliban. President Karzai insists that only those Taliban who are willing to give up arms will be amnestied; those that are still violently opposing the government would be held accountable. But making deals with the Taliban, particularly from a position of weakness, is a bad idea. The key to restoring peace and stability in Afghanistan does not lie in extending concessions to violent extremists but in meeting the genuine grievances of the population. Taliban leaders appear least interested in dialogue. Even if they were, amnesty for hardcore Taliban leaders and commanders and inclusion in government would send the message that the road to power in present-day Afghanistan is through the gun. Negotiating with spoilers is unlikely to stabilise Afghanistan. It will far more likely undermine state authority and legitimacy, and could take Afghanistan back to civil war and the anarchy that made the country a haven for criminals and local, regional, and transnational terrorists.

---

[14] See International Crisis Group, *Reforming Afghanistan's Police*, Report No. 138, August 23, 2007.

[15] International Crisis Group, *Countering Afghanistan's Insurgency* (2006, p. 21).

CHAPTER TEN

Afghanistan: Prospects for Nation Building

Ali Jalali[1]

The process of state building in Afghanistan is influenced by diverging concepts that underpin the policies of domestic, regional, and global actors playing on the Afghan political scene.

Internationally Assisted State Building

International involvement in the state-building process was initiated as an afterthought to the fight against global terrorism, and was driven by the desire to remove the threat to the United States emanating from Afghan territory. The prime reason for the U.S. military intervention in Afghanistan was to destroy the terrorist network responsible for the 9/11 attack and to topple the Taliban regime. Although international efforts to stabilize post-Taliban Afghanistan are considered a strategic objective in the global war on terror, the operational exigencies of military action continue to cast a long shadow on the state-building process in the war-devastated country. Local and regional allies that the United States picked for their counterterrorism schemes have their own agendas and often do not contribute to building peace and stability in Afghanistan. Additionally, in the initial phase of the war and immediately after the conflict, the level of investment in reconstructing Afghanistan was determined not by the actual needs of the country but rather shaped by the requirements of military operations—an inauspicious way to create a modern state. This has been a low-cost military intervention and a cheap state-building endeavor.

In-Conflict Reconstruction

Unlike the conflict in the Balkans and Iraq, the conflict in Afghanistan is not caused by deep-seated hostility fueled by religious, ethnic, and linguistic differences. Afghanistan conflict is mostly the result of foreign influence. Ethnic, sectarian, and linguistic tensions during the conflict were the result, not the cause, of the civil war.

Nevertheless, the state-building effort is taking place amid a cycle of violence that has deep roots in the region, as well as in Afghanistan's immediate past. Unlike many other cases of nation building, including Bosnia and Kosovo, state building in Afghanistan is conducted in an environment in which competing demands for a response to immediate security needs

[1] Ali Jalali, former Interior Minister of Afghanistan (January 2003–September 2005), is currently serving as both a distinguished professor at the Near East South Asia Center for Strategic Studies (NESA) and as a researcher at the Institute for National Strategic Studies (INSS).

and the requirements of long-term priorities are often hard to reconcile, even though they can be mutually reinforcing.

There are two other important factors that influence the process of state building in Afghanistan: the country's history and a socio-political transformation in the country resulting from war.

The Legacy of History

The terms *nation building* and *state building* are often used interchangeably in contemporary parlance. But the contrast between the two processes in Afghanistan is manifest. Despite experiencing a long period of instability and violence, nation building in Afghanistan is not an issue, while state building is a major challenge. Afghanistan has a strong nation and a weak state. In the recent past, the Afghan nation has shown surprising strength and viability with no trace of secessionist calls, threats, or attempts.

But the development of a modern state in Afghanistan has been extremely slow. Disadvantaged by restricted political, military, and financial resources, as well as geographic constraints, the central governments in Afghanistan historically exercised loose control over the country's regions and governed them through local leaders who either received special privileges from the state or were balanced against each other. A centralized state coexisted with a fragmented, decentralized traditional society, and the interplay between the two has been one of the recurrent themes in modern history.

This historical decentralization of governance has spawned a wide system of traditional power structures, norms, and practices that cannot be ignored in building a modern state in Afghanistan.

The Impact of War

In addition to the enormous human loss and material destruction, the long years of war and violence changed the fabric of the society and upset the traditional alignment of political forces in the country. Three interconnected domestic factors were responsible for the landmark transformation: a crisis of legitimacy, a failure to substitute destroyed state institutions with new ones, and a rise of sub-state powers.

The breakdown of central authority and war-instigated socio-political transformation further vitalized the regional patronage networks under the leadership of regional commanders who often invoked ethnic references to legitimize their leadership. This situation has stimulated ethno-regional competition for power and resource distribution.

Centralization or Decentralization

Neither adopting traditional structures as substitutes for modern state institutions nor an excessive decentralization of power is a suitable response to the current challenges. The state building process needs to reconcile these realities with the requirements of a stable state in Afghanistan. Long-term stability in Afghanistan requires that efforts be directed toward changing the divisive situation rather than adopting solutions solely to accommodate the existing fragmentation. Accommodation of traditional power structures and different ethnic groups has to be sought through democratic participation, political and economic integration, and the development of a civil society and private sector that mitigate the negative impacts of competing group interests.

Removal of existing perceptional and managerial distance between Kabul and the regions is essential for the de-fragmentation of governance. The key to this is bringing a balance between creating a strong and effective central government and ensuring a level of decentralization to secure equal distribution of resources and participation. One of the challenges is the degree to which administrative and fiscal authorities are delegated to sub-national governments.

Conclusion

The challenge of state building in Afghanistan is complex and multifaceted. Although the U.S. war on terror has a regional dimension and requires a regional approach, Afghanistan cannot achieve stability unless the regional aspects of violence are addressed effectively.

Building a stable and effective modern state in Afghanistan requires a long-term commitment by the international community to invest in addressing both short- and long-term needs. The strategy should aim to end the insurgency and to create effective governance systems capable of establishing the rule of law, providing human security and public services, and fostering economic development that can replace the illicit drug trade with legal economic activities.

CHAPTER ELEVEN

How to Create Success for the Afghan National Security Forces

Peter Dahl Thruelsen[1]

Within the concept of nation building, the elements of security sector reform have become an issue of importance at the same level as building democratic institutions and conducting elections. Security sector reforms in the context of post-conflict environments have to be seen as the guarantee for a stable and prosperous development of peace and stability in any post-conflict setting. Today in Afghanistan we—the international community and the Afghan government—are conducting both counterinsurgency operations in the southern and eastern parts of Afghanistan and more traditional peacekeeping operations in the northern and western part of the country.

There is no doubt that the fight for a more stable and prosperous Afghanistan will be determined in the southern and eastern parts of the country and that it will be settled by the will, determination, commitment, and long-term focus of the international community. The long-term focus will have to be guided by a holistic strategy encompassing both capabilities and capacities of the Afghan government. One of the main efforts in conducting a counterinsurgency campaign is to create a legitimate host nation that is capable of addressing the root causes of the conflict[2]. If root causes are not addressed, the insurgents will use them to gain momentum and to undermine the legitimacy of the host nation. This again will be used by the insurgents to gain support amongst the civil population. There are of course many elements in creating a legitimate host nation and in creating the capacity to actually address the root causes of the conflict. Elements of creating a government that actively can support the population by providing basic services such as health care, jobs and economic progress, justice, law and order, etc., are critical. However, legitimacy in the eyes of the people basically is a question of the ability of the government to exercise its sovereignty independently throughout the country—without the help of external actors. If the government of the host nation that is conducting counterinsurgency operations has neither the capacity nor the capability to counter the insurgency, its legitimacy in the eyes of the population will crumble. If the host nation is perceived as a marionette puppet by the local population, not capable of being in charge of its own country, the support will crumble. This will mobilize support behind the insurgents, whose strength will rise.[3]

---

[1] Peter Dahl Thruelsen is a research fellow at the Institute for Strategy at the Royal Danish Defence College. His main area of research is conflict resolution, nation building, security sector reform, and peacekeeping/enforcement. The author can be contacted by email at ifs-71@fak.dk.

[2] Headquarters, Department of the Army, *Counterinsurgency*, Field Manual 3-24, Washington, D.C., June 2006, p. 6-1.

[3] John A. Nagl, *Learning to Eat Soup with a Knife: Counterinsurgency Lessons from Malaya and Vietnam*, New York: Praeger, 2002, p. 76.

Forming capabilities within a new government administration is a huge task that must not to be led by the military. An effective, noncorrupt, and legitimate administration is a precondition for building a legitimate capability—the executive power—within the state. One of the greatest challenges towards capacity building within the Afghan government is the immersive corruption problems infiltrating all levels of the new administration, making many institutions and procedures dysfunctional. On the other hand, building the security capabilities of a new government administration definitely is a task for the military. The main capabilities of the executive power currently being built within the security institutions in Afghanistan are the Afghan National Army (ANA) and the Afghan National Police (ANP).

My argument in this paper will be that corruption needs to be tackled primarily on the highest national and provincial level in order to make the officers and civil servants in the field realise that corruption is damaging and will be punished. Furthermore, the mistrust towards ANP should be countered by changing the deployment structures within ANP, so that the police officers do not work in the provinces from where they originate. To enhance the effectiveness of these efforts, a mentor and liaison programme equivalent to the ANA programme will be crucial for success of ANP. Furthermore, the fact is that the local population in Afghanistan is waiting to see who the strongest party is, and is waiting to see whether or not the Afghan government and thereby Afghan National Security Forces can deal with the immense security challenges in the country. Therefore we need to help create the successes for them—especially the ANA—and to establish the win-win scenario that will demonstrate to the civilian population that the Afghan security forces can take charge of security independently of international forces. The win-win scenario could be the northern part of Afghanistan.

Building Afghan National Security Forces

The concept of security sector reform has many variants, depending on the different context of implementation and political processes leading to implementation. Security sector reform in Afghanistan is divided into five pillars, each with a lead nation responsible for implementation of the reform. The five pillars are military reform, police reform, judicial reform, counternarcotics, and disarmament. In this paper, the two pillars concerning military reform and police reform will be analysed.

Afghan National Army

The rebuilding of the ANA was started in May 2002 by U.S. forces. Overall, the rebuilding programme can be characterised as a success within the framework of security sector reform, especially in relation to the rebuilding of the ANP and in relation to the similar programmes conducted in Africa and in Iraq. Today, approximately 42,000 soldiers[4] out of a projected total of 70,000 by 2010[5] have been trained and deployed to the provinces, and the project to make

---

[4] Islamic Republic of Afghanistan, Afghanistan National Development Strategy Joint Coordination and Monitoring Board, *Annual Report*, May 2007, Annex II, "The Year in Review—Key Sectory Achievements, Challenges, and Priorities." Of the 42,000, some 6,000–8,000 are currently in basic training.

[5] Islamic Republic of Afghanistan, *Afghan National Development Strategy, Vol. I*, undated, pp. 70–71.

the ANA a sustainable force is progressing positively.[6] Its overall success can be seen in the light of the high level of training and the generally positive response of the civilian population towards the ANA when it has been deployed to the provinces.

Most parts of the basic training for the new ANA recruits are being conducted in Kabul by Afghan officers and instructors together with the U.S. Task Force Phoenix,[7] which consists of some 2,000 U.S. personnel. The quality of recruited personnel varies, with the majority being illiterate and in bad health. The target, however, of approximately 2,000 new recruits per month in spring 2007 has been met. Once ANA soldiers have gone through basic training, they are deployed to a region for active duty, where they work closely with international forces, who train, exercise, and conduct patrols and operations in close cooperation with them. When deployed to a region, an ANA unit is paired with an advisory unit of international military personnel called an Operational Mentoring and Liaison Team (OMLT). The OMLT consists of international officers and noncommissioned officers who follow ANA units from the platoon level all the way to brigade level and on to the Afghan Ministry of Defence. When deployed together, the OMLT mentors and trains the ANA unit both in the military camps and during combat operations.

The OMLT system is quite essential for the success of the ANA in training, during operations, and in the effort to reach the end state: a sustainable ANA. There are, however, some huge challenges with the system that need to be addressed if the success enjoyed so far is to continue. The advisors following the ANA units are under tremendous stress to constantly train and further educate the ANA soldiers before, during, and after operations. This is something that is continuously being challenged by the complexity of the fighting in especially southern and eastern Afghanistan and by the ever-changing nature of the insurgency. Also, the U.S.-led Task Force Phoenix is planning to reduce its commitment to the training of the ANA and instead change its focus to mentoring the ANP. These challenges will foster a need for more OMLT personnel from ISAF and eventually the need for a new lead nation for the whole programme.

The U.S. intention to change the focus of Task Force Phoenix from the ANA to the ANP seems sound. The ANP—as will be seen below—has massive obstacles to its becoming a reliable and trustworthy police force. Therefore, the United States will deploy National Guard instructors with a civilian police education to Afghanistan to strengthen the currently underdeveloped ANP programme. For the United States to reallocate resources and to be able to change focus, they need ISAF to take over the control of the current ANA programme and to enhance its commitment to the OMLT system. The United States has asked ISAF-participating nations to take the lead, but at the time of this writing (June 2007) no nation has replied positively. Also, to push the ANA educational programme, U.S. Task Force Phoenix is planning to shorten the length of the centrally conducted basic training programme in Kabul, with the dual purpose of reaching 70,000 by the end of 2008 instead of 2010 and getting more troops through the programme and deployed to the regional commands. This will further advance the need for additional OMLT in the regions if the training standard and operational preparedness is to be maintained at present levels. If the extra need for OMLT is not met, it must be expected that the current operational success with ANA will be damaged.

---

6 ANA Corps HQ is in: Mazae-i-Sharif 209 Corp, Heart 207 Corp, Kandahar 205 Corp, Gradez 203 Corp, and Kabul 201 Corp.

7 For more on Combined Joint Task Force Phoenix, see http://www.floridaguard.army.mil/tfphoenix/default.asp

Today, on the tactical level, the ANA seems to be performing its duties professionally in the field and when it is involved in larger operations with the international forces. Generally, the fighting spirit seems high, morale is good, and most soldiers perform professionally. For some years now, the ANA has been quite an important element in creating stability and security throughout the country; however, there is still a long way for the ANA to go before it is able to take over the tasks of the international forces. The greatest challenge facing the ANA seems to be institutional, that is, how to professionalize and transform itself into an independent and sustainable actor. When the United States started the ANA rebuilding programme, it emphasised the need to give the training programme sufficient time in order to create effective fighting units. This approach has proved to be successful in relation to ANA professional conduct. The downside of the approach, however, has been that the number of trained troops going through the programme has been far less than needed. The consequences of the low training rate are many. First, the ANA is in no position to take over the demanding security tasks of the country. Second, it cannot support the provincial governors with troops even in the more stable areas. Third, the ANA seems to have become somewhat run down because of the heavy fighting it has been engaged in and the lack of reinforcements. Recent reports from the southern and eastern parts of the country have shown that the demands on the ANA are so heavy that units do not have time to rebuild their strength between battles. As a result, the rate of desertion is rising in these regions, with almost 20 percent[8] of soldiers deployed having gone absent.

Afghan National Police

The rebuilding of the ANP under German leadership commenced in April 2002. The primary focus of the programme has been to rebuild the Police Academy in Kabul and to create a three-year police officer education programme. However, it soon became obvious that the German effort put into the programme was not enough, and that a large-scale basic training programme was needed if the police were to manage the security situation in the country. The fact is that only a very limited number of German police officers have been stationed in Afghanistan to lead the rebuilding, and it underscores that that too few resources have been allocated. In 2003, training programmes for regular police officers were initiated through training centres around the country. The basic training centres were led by the United States, who also began to finance different kinds of individual police equipment. The United States contracted the private contractor Dyncorp International to be in charge of the training centres, and by 2006 one central training centre in Kabul and seven centres in the regions were operational. At the time of this writing, the programme to strengthen the Ministry of Internal Affairs and to rebuild the ANP cannot be characterised as a success. Today, the goal of training 62,000 police officers[9] has generally been met but with a lot of emphasis on quantity rather than quality. The consequence is that only some 30,000 of the ANP officers are somewhat capable of performing police duties.[10] Overall, the training programme of the ANP does not seem to be based

---

8 Combined Security Transition Command Afghanistan (CSTC-A), April 2007.

9 Islamic Republic of Afghanistan, *Afghan National Development Strategy, Vol. I*, undated, pp. 70–71.

10 Inspectors General, U.S. Departments of State and Defense, *Interagency Assessment of Afghanistan Police Training and Readiness*, Report No. ISP-IQO-07-07, 2006, p. 15.

on a comprehensive analysis of the actual security situation in the country, and as a result the ANP have sustained a high level of casualties. Also, the ANP is beset with corruption, which is garnering it the general mistrust of the local population. The principal problems here are the lack of training to cope with the security situation and the difficulties that corruption creates for cooperation with ISAF, primarily because ISAF does not trust ANP officers. All problems point to the urgent need to improve the quality of the police force.

Corruption within the ANP primarily takes the form of bribes, due to low wages, local loyalties, and also personal clan relations in the districts in which police officers are stationed. The average police officer is recruited in the district he is to serve in. As just noted, the scale of corruption affects the effectiveness and credibility of the ANP in the eyes of the civil population. Therefore, the ANP is not perceived as an actor that can be trusted to implement and maintain security, authority, and rule of law in the provinces.[11] In interviews conducted in Afghanistan in 2006 and 2007, I was presented with the dilemma that international support for the ANP is in some instances seen by the local population as direct support for the repressive and criminal elements in society, which hardly consolidates the work of ISAF. Also, civilians sometimes express greater confidence in the Taliban than the ANP because the Taliban does not collect bribes or collect special taxes at checkpoints.

In summer 2006, President Karzai ordered the establishment of an auxiliary police force that is to be activated in the especially fragile districts of eastern and southern Afghanistan.[12] The initiative soon became knows as the Afghan National Auxiliary Police (ANAP). It was from the beginning deemed controversial, but nevertheless the initiative is now being implemented. The primary reason for the ANAP to be established was the security situation, which began to deteriorate in fall 2005 to spring 2006. At the time it was estimated that an additional 20,000 police officers would be needed to handle the security challenges the country faced. These extra officers could not, however, be formed from within the current ANP programme, because of the international agreements on a 62,000-strong police force. Security assessments dividing Afghanistan into three security zones (11 provinces as high threat, 9 provinces as medium threat, and 14 provinces as low threat) came up with an assessment that a minimum of 20,000 additional police are needed.[13]

Currently approximately 5,000 ANAP officers have gone through the new programme set up to train and equip the new police officers. A new police officer under the ANAP system receives a 10-day education focusing on the very basic elements required to conduct official duties. Upon finishing the training programme, the new ANAP officer signs a one-year contract and receives an ANP uniform, a Kalashnikov rifle, and the same salary as an ordinary ANP officer. The officer is then deployed to a high-risk district, normally from where he originates, to perform police duties. Table 11.1 shows the status of ANAP training as of April 2007.

On a professional level, the ANP is not able to handle the extreme demands that the current security situation presents. Also, on the issue of police officer salary, the ANP has immense problems. An officer in the ANP and ANAP receives $70 US a month, which is considerably below calculated living costs for an average Afghan family. Also, $70 US a month is $30 US

---

11 Inspectors General (2006, pp. 15–16).

12 On August 16, 2006, President Karzai presented ten objectives in a directive to strengthen development in the country. Objective no. 7 establishes the ADZs.

13 Islamic Republic of Afghanistan, Afghanistan National Development Strategy Joint Coordination and Monitoring Board, *JCMB Task Force on Afghan National Police Target Strength*, March 2007.

Table 11.1
Status of ANAP Training

Area	Authorised	Trained
South: Helmand, Kandahar, Nimroz, Uruzgan, Zabul, Daykonid	5,351	3,840
East: Ghazni, Khost, Paktia, Paktika	2,450	748
West: Farah, Ghor, Heart	660	267
North: Faryab	100	0
Central: Kapisa, Kunar, Laghman, Logar, Nangarhar, Nuristan, Wardak	2,700	82

SOURCE: ISAF HQ Kabul, April 2007

below the comparable wage level within the ANA. Another problem with salaries in the ANP is the actual payment of the police officers. Currently, there is no functioning banking system from where the salaries can be paid out, which is why salaries often are paid hand to hand by a government official or an international representative.

The system is obviously not effective and contributes to corruption, especially in the form of young officers being forced to give higher-ranking officers some of their payroll. The inadequate salary payment system also leads to attrition because of lack of payments. The attrition rate is currently around 15 percent. In a recent example from Daykondi Province, 89 ANAP officers abandoned their posts after not having received salary in up to five months. An additional 65 ANP and ANAP officers threatened to leave their posts in the same province for the same reason.

Conclusion

Implementing security sector reform in Afghanistan is a complex and costly process that will require a long-term and genuine commitment by the international community. If this commitment and the resources are not made available, Afghanistan will not be able to take charge of Afghanistan. Instead, the international community will be caught in a vicious circle, reacting to developments instead of preempting them. Therefore, it is of utmost importance that the mission's broader goal is not lost in the short tactical victories or the cost of reaching the strategic end state.

Afghan National Police

The education and training programme of the ANP must be structured so that it reflects the actual security situation in the country. It has to be strengthened from a central place, so that all new police officers can manage the challenges as a united and trustworthy unit. Corruption needs to be tackled, primarily on the highest national and provincial levels in order to make officers in the field realise that corruption will be punished. Furthermore, the mistrust towards the ANP should be countered by changing the deployment structures within the ANP, so that police officers do not work in the provinces from where they originate. To enhance the effectiveness of these efforts, a mentor and liaison programme equivalent to the ANA programme will be crucial for the success of the ANP. Therefore, joint efforts should be undertaken to strengthen the education and day-to-day performance of the ANP, with training teams in the provinces and embedded advisors attached to the ANP in the districts. The reform programme should encompass all elements of reforming state security apparatus, including reforming the Ministry of Interior, pay structures, training and equipment, and adjusting the rank structures together with rule of law in a modern state. Also, to enhance the efficiency and to fight corruption, the deployment of ANP officers needs to be prioritised with respect to the security situation, and the deployed officers should be deployed to provinces other than one they call home, or they should at least be part of a rotation system.

Afghan National Army

The educational rate of the ANA must be strengthened if it is to take over the security tasks in the country. The education frequency should not be increased on the basis of lesser educational demands, but rather by increasing the number of international and national instructors to train the units. This will enable more units to go through the programme with the same high educational level. The increased efforts should be focused on both the basic training in Kabul and the specialised training in the regions. This should reinforce the Afghan state in its efforts to gain a monopoly on power, and it will create a sustainable ANA in the current operational involvement. However, with the United States refocusing its efforts to strengthen the training and education of the ANP, ISAF should take over the responsibility for the centrally led ANA training, and it should enhance its efforts in regard to the OMLT system. If the generally positive development of the ANA is to continue and if the ANA is to handle the complex and ever-changing insurgency operating in the country, a reinforced OMLT system needs to be created. In this regard, the demand for more instructors and mentors should to some extent be filled by the more combat-reluctant NATO countries.

To minimise the attrition of the ANA and to enhance the perceptions of the ANA in the civil population as well as the general perception of the future, it should be asked whether the ANA should be put in charge of some of the more stable provinces in the country, such as Regional Command North and eventually Regional Command West, thus freeing ISAF units for security, stability, instructor, mentoring, or development tasks. This could strengthen the ANA in the eyes of the local population and move forward the process of handing the country back to the Afghans themselves, which is ultimately the end state. The fact is that the local population in Afghanistan is waiting to see who the strongest party is, and waiting to see whether or not the Afghan government and the Afghan National Security Forces can handle the immense security challenges in the country. Therefore we need to help with creating successes and establishing the win-win scenario that will demonstrate to the civilian population that the Afghan security forces can take charge of security independently of the international forces—especially after the international forces have left. The win-win scenario could be the northern part of Afghanistan.

CHAPTER TWELVE

Afghanistan at the Crossroads

Obaid Younossi and Khalid Nadiri[1]

Background

Afghanistan is a landlocked country of approximately 250,000 square miles located at the intersection of the Iranian Plateau, the Central Asian Steppes, and the Indian subcontinent. It is bordered by Iran in the west, Pakistan in the south and east, Turkmenistan, Uzbekistan, and Tajikistan in the north, and China in its easternmost region. Its estimated population of 30 million consists of several major ethnic groups and is predominantly Muslim—around 80 percent Sunni and 19 percent Shi'a.[2]

Modern Afghan history has been marked by conflict, instability, and frequent changes in power, due in part to its strategic location, independent clan structure, and wide-ranging ethnic and cultural-linguistic composition. Since its founding in 1747 by Ahmad Shah Durrani, Afghanistan has seen three Anglo-Afghan wars, the 1979 Soviet invasion and ensuing insurgency, several years of civil war during the 1990s, and the authoritarian regime of the ultraconservative Islamist Taliban.

The September 11, 2001, attacks against the United States precipitated the ouster of the Taliban and the establishment of the Bonn Agreement, a U.N.-sponsored process of reconciliation, reconstruction, and self-government meant to promote lasting peace and sustained development of Afghanistan's economy and institutions.

Progress has been visible. In the last five years, Afghanistan's licit economy has grown at an average of 15 percent in real terms.[3] Primary school enrollment has increased six-fold[4] and female labor force participation continues to rise. At the same time, Afghanistan has inaugurated its first democratically elected president and a bicameral parliament.

In spite of the progress, Afghanistan remains a fragile state, and public optimism is waning (see Figure 12.1). Taliban and al Qaeda militants carry out strikes in eastern and southern Afghanistan with greater deadliness and frequency, many of which are launched from Pakistan. Local militias and the Taliban itself have been able to extend or maintain their control of large parts of the Afghan countryside, which is used to finance their operations through the cultivation of poppy. Further, despite strong economic growth over the past

1 Obaid Younossi is a senior management scientist at the RAND Corporation and Khalid Nadiri is a former analyst at the RAND Corporation and currently a graduate student at SAIS, Johns Hopkins University.

2 Central Intelligence Agency, "Afghanistan," in *The World Factbook*, 2005.

3 International Monetary Fund, "IMF Board Approves $119.1 Million PRGF Arrangement for the Islamic Republic of Afghanistan," June 26, 2006.

4 United Nations Children's Fund, "Millions of Afghan Children Head Back to School," March 21, 2007.

Figure 12.1
Positive Ratings of the United States in Afghanistan

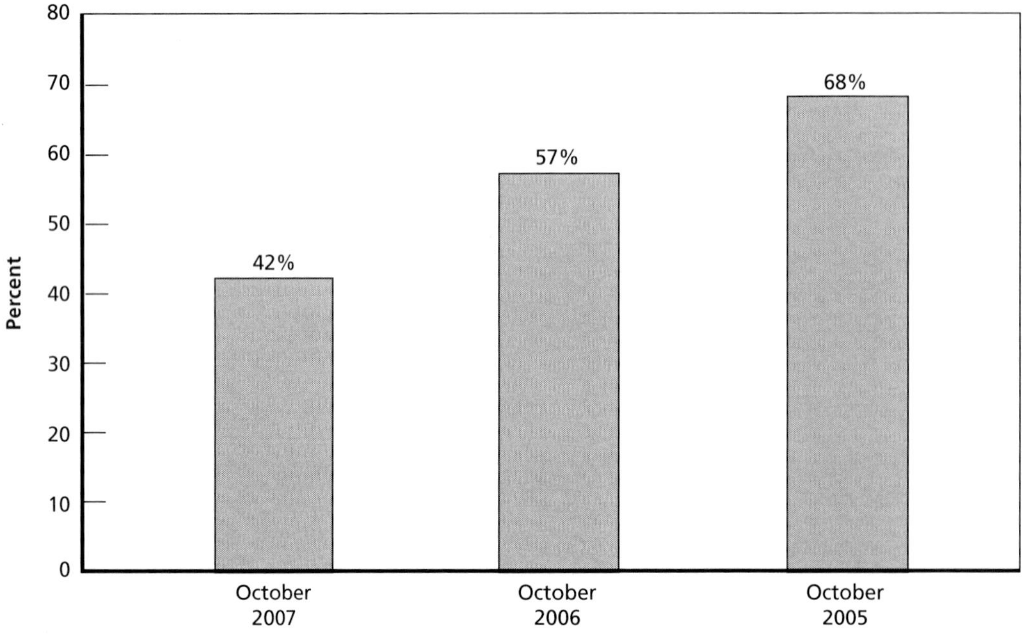

SOURCE: ABC News/BBC World Service Poll, "Afghanistan: Where Things Stand," December 2007.
RAND *CF238-12.1*

five years, Afghanistan remains one of the poorest countries in the world, and its government is not able to provide jobs and services for a growing and increasingly frustrated population. The entrenchment and interconnectedness of these obstacles are a long-term challenge for the Afghan government and the international community.

This paper summarizes the major Afghan concerns and provides some recommendations to policymakers on what should be done.

Threats to Security

Afghanistan faces three major security threats: terrorists, insurgents, and criminals. The lines of delineation among these three groups blur. The number of Taliban and al Qaeda attacks against U.S., NATO, and Afghan security forces as well as civilians rose throughout 2006, along with the sophistication of the tactics and weaponry used in them.[5] In 2006 alone, more than 3,700 Afghans fell victim to Taliban attacks—a four-fold increase over 2005. This occurred despite the fact that 20,000 U.S. troops and 20,000 additional soldiers from other NATO nations are stationed in Afghanistan. The south and east of Afghanistan have experienced the highest incidence of attacks, largely because the Pashtun-dominated Taliban enjoy some popularity among the majority Pashtun population there and in the Northwestern Frontier Province of Pakistan,

---

[5] United Nations, *Secretary-General Report to the UN Security Council on the Situation in Afghanistan and Its Implications for International Peace and Security*, 2005.

which is frequently used as a safe haven. A 2006 survey of the Afghans by the Asia Foundation, shown in Figure 12.2, suggests that lack of security ranks as the Afghans' top concern.

Disarmament of the Armed Factions

Japan was the lead nation responsible for the Disarmament, Demobilization, and Reintegration (DDR) of Afghan Military Forces (AMF). In June of 2005, all armed organizations were either disarmed or integrated into the ANA. Some 10,000 heavy weapons and 31,000 light weapons were collected. Almost 67,000 formerly armed people were transitioned to civilian life. Under the Disarmament of Illegal Armed Groups (DIAG), 20,000 weapons were turned in voluntarily. A U.N. official stated that some armed factions were not disarmed because the Afghan government and the international forces were unable to fill the security vacuum created through the disarmament.[6]

The July 2005 completion of the AMF disarmament program[7] was not completely successful. High-profile government commanders and corrupt government officials connected to nonstatutory militias were not dealt with by the Afghan government because pursuing them

Figure 12.2
Top Concern of Afghans

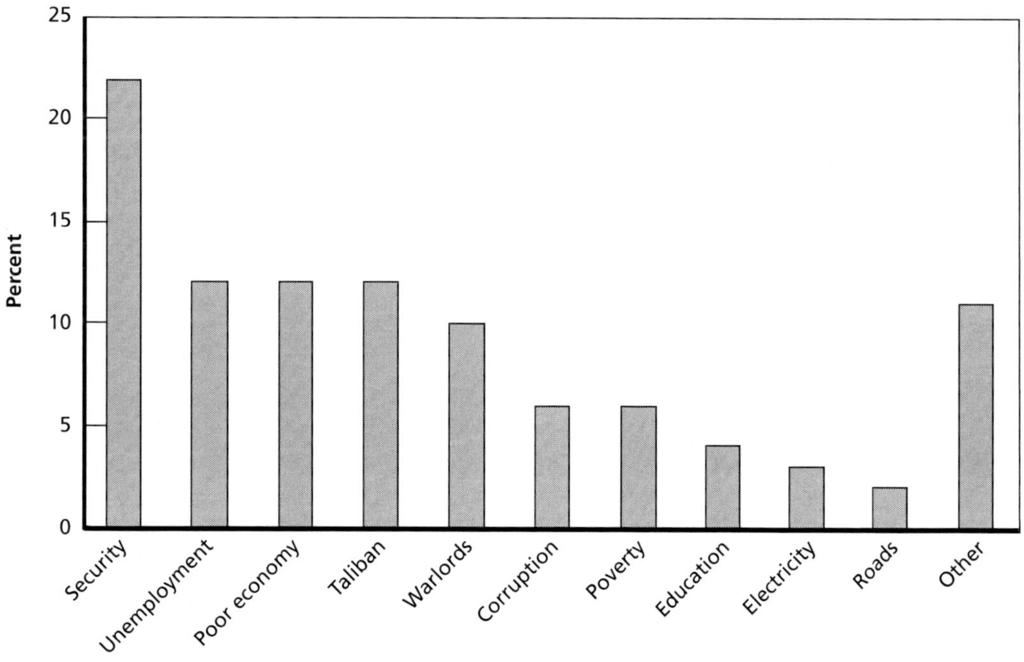

SOURCE: Asia Foundation, *Afghanistan in 2006: A Survey of the Afghan People*, Kabul, Afghanistan, 2006.
NOTE: Respondents were asked, "In your view, what is the biggest problem facing Afghanistan as a whole?" and were allowed to select two answers.
RAND *CF238-12.2*

[6] Author's discussion with a UN official in Kabul.

[7] Author's discussion with a UN official in Kabul.

was seen as risky.[8] Significant numbers of light weapons remain in the country. Warlords and their private militias remain armed, well funded, and numerous. It is estimated that 1,800 armed bands consisting of 100,000 individuals roam the Afghan countryside. Zalmai Rassoul, the National Security Advisor, best summarized the issue of illegal armed groups and their effect on the rule of law during his address to the ISAF Provincial Reconstruction Team's commander conference on November 6, 2005:

> The illegal armed groups, and there are far too many, pose a threat to good governance generally, and more specifically to the extension of the rule of law and the writ of central government into the provinces. While illegal armed groups continue to roam unencumbered by any respect for the law, corruption will remain widespread and our counter-narcotic strategies are unlikely to succeed.

Figure 12.3, from the RAND-MIPT Terrorist Incident Database, shows a steady increase in the number of attacks (dashed line) and number of fatalities caused (solid line) by insurgents. Interestingly, the number of fatalities caused by insurgents increased faster than the number of attacks, suggesting that terrorist tactics and weaponry are getting more sophisticated and lethal.

Figure 12.3
Rise in Number of Attacks and Fatalities

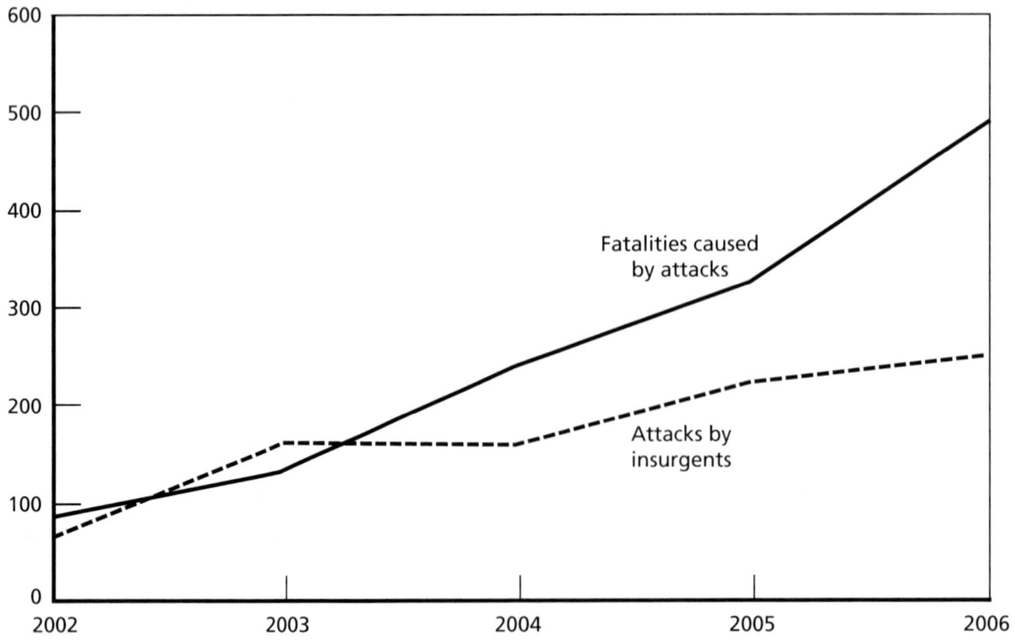

SOURCE: RAND-MIPT Terrorist Incident Database.
RAND *CF238-12.3*

---

[8] United Nations Development Programme, *Afghanistan's New Beginning Programme 2005 Third Quarter Report*, AFG/03/Mo5/ND/34.

Opium Production

Afghanistan remains the largest source of opium in the world. Poppy cultivation and opium production have increased dramatically in 2007, rising 17 percent and 34 percent, respectively. While poppy cultivation is widespread, it has become increasingly concentrated in southern Afghanistan in the last two years, particularly in Helmand province (see figure 12.4). Helmand, most of which is controlled by the Taliban, accounted for 50 percent of Afghanistan's entire opium crop in 2007. Together with four other southern provinces that share a border with Pakistan, that share rises to 70 percent.

Poppy cultivation and opium production make up the largest proportion of Afghanistan's GDP. According to the Afghanistan Opium Survey 2005, published by the United Nations Office on Drugs and Crime, the estimated number of hectares of poppy under cultivation for 2007 was 193,000 hectares,[9] up from 165,000 hectares in 2006. Opium production has continued to grow rapidly in the last six years, standing at more than twice its average in the 1990s (see Figure 12.5).

Figure 12.4
Opium Cultivation by Province, 2006

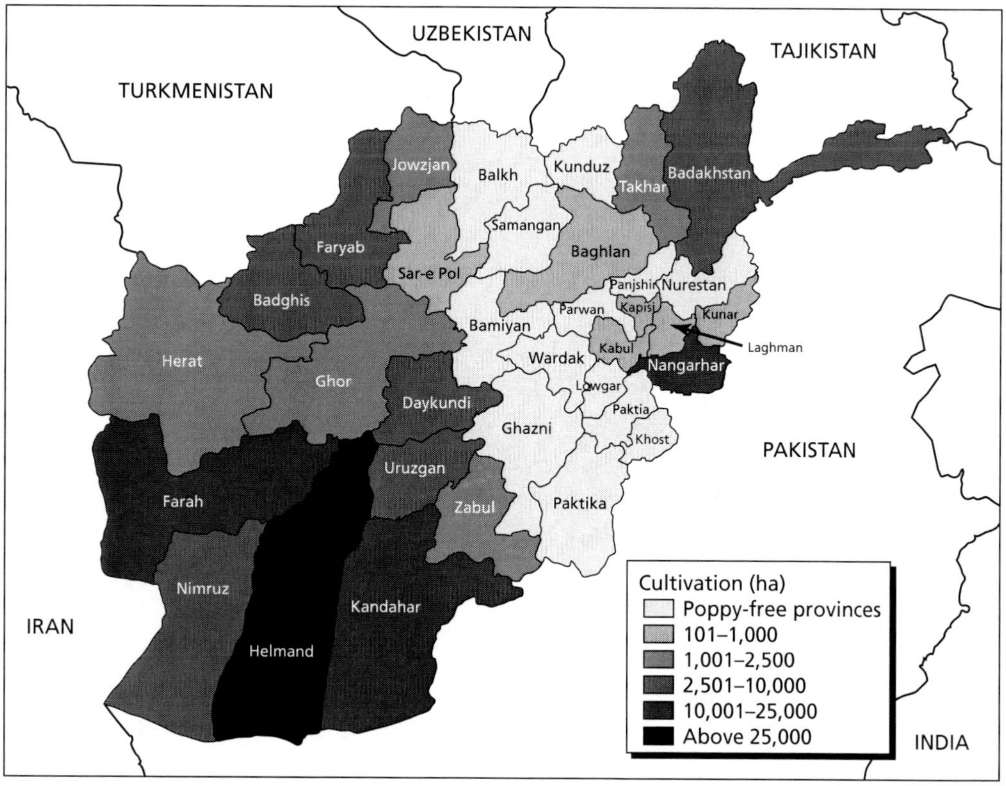

SOURCE: United Nations Office on Drugs and Crime, *Afghanistan Opium Survey*, 2007.
RAND *CF238-12.4*

[9] United Nations Office on Drugs and Crime, *Afghanistan Opium Survey 2007*, August 2007.

Figure 12.5
Tons of Poppy Produced by Year

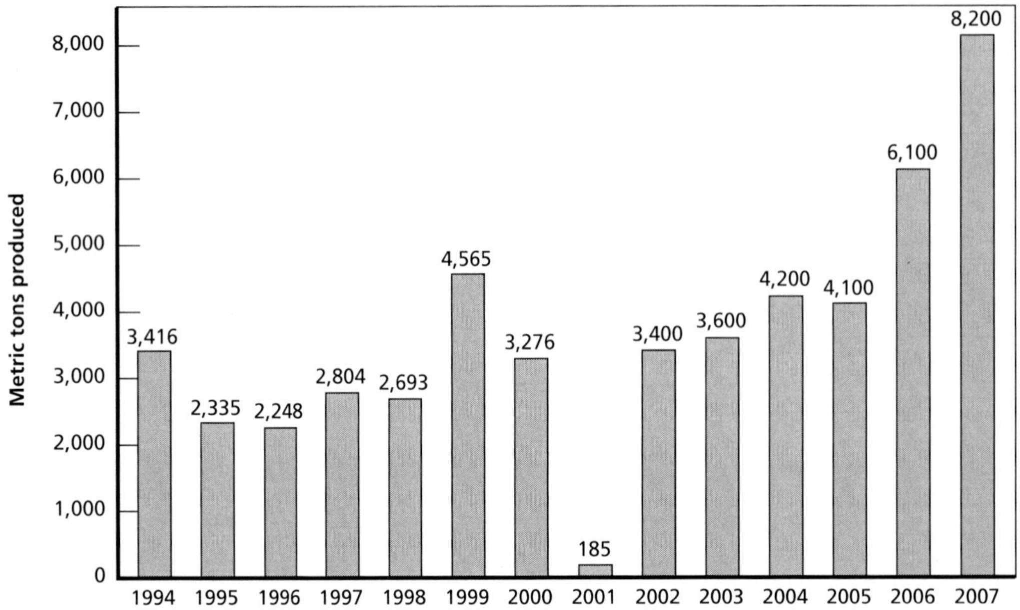

SOURCE: United Nations Office on Drugs and Crime, 2006.
RAND *CF238-12.5*

Many of the proceeds of Afghanistan's poppy trade finance criminal activities and the insurgency and effectively stunt the development of Afghanistan's licit economy. Even some senior government officials are allegedly engaged in the drug trade.[10] However, most Afghans who participated in the recent 2006 ABC News/BBC World Service polls did not see poppy cultivation as a concern (see figure 12.6).

Major drug trafficking groups in Afghanistan have amassed considerable fortunes. Even though opium production has decreased this year, significant stockpiles exist. Seven provinces make up the largest percentage of poppy producers (Badakhshan, Nangarhar, Balkh, Urozgan, Farah, Kandahar, and Helmand). There is some evidence of cooperation between opium producer/traffickers and Taliban forces. Afghan traffickers are mostly in control in Afghanistan, and foreigners handle the international drug trade from Afghanistan. Pakistani traffickers are much more sophisticated. Twenty percent of drugs produced in Afghanistan are transported through the west (Herat) to Iran, 10 percent to Tajikistan through the north, and the remaining 70 percent through the south to Pakistan. Forces from the United Kingdom have led many of Afghanistan's narcotics control efforts, with the United States fully engaging with them in their efforts.

---

10 "Afghanistan Riddled with Drug Ties," *Christian Science Monitor*, May 13, 2005

Figure 12.6
Afghani Attitudes Regarding Poppy Production

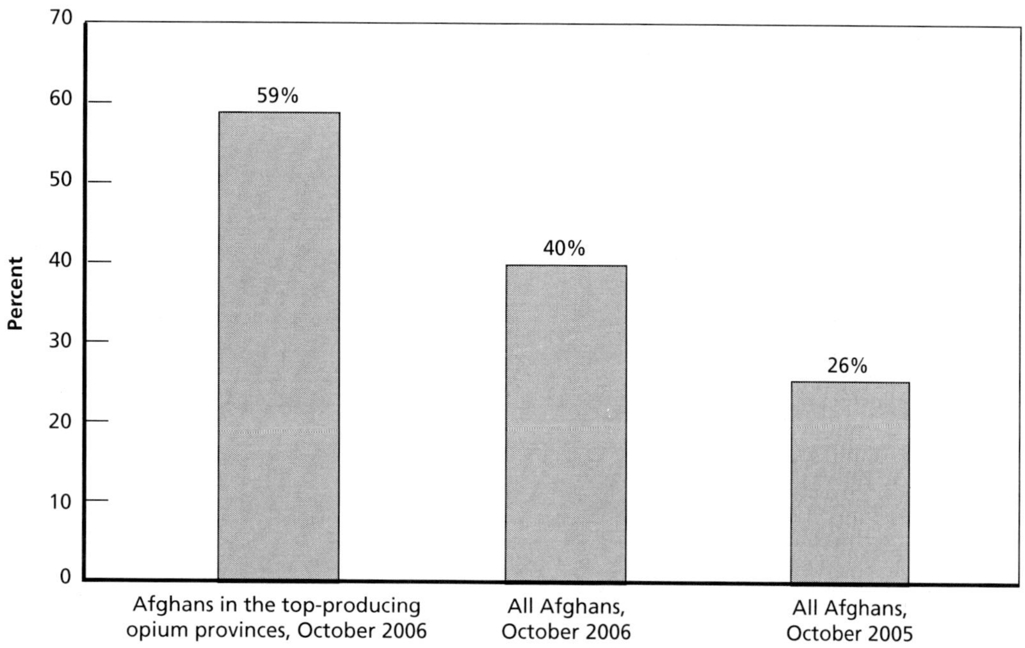

SOURCE: ABC News/BBC World Service Poll, "Afghanistan: Where Things Stand," December 2007.
RAND *CF238-12.6*

Corruption and Capacity Building

According to Freedom House, addressing corruption and transparency have taken somewhat of a backseat to more pressing issues such as improving security, the rule of law, economic opportunities, and access to health and education. Consequently, corruption continues to permeate the Afghan government. By and large, there is an absence of any sense of accountability by government officials, in large part because many feel that they hold their offices only temporarily. Hence, they are building a "nest egg" for the future. Institution-building efforts led by various countries according to the Bonn Agreement among the donor nations is progressing slowly. For example, little progress has been made to establish a functioning justice system and reform the Afghan National Police (ANP). Questions on whether the justice system will be based on a Western model or on a traditional Afghan model remain largely unanswered. Many of those involved in the reform of the ANP complained that there might not be any laws in time to fine or imprison criminals once arrests are made. An absence of any system of accountability for monitoring resources allocated for various nationwide projects only facilitates the corruption.

The pace of reconstruction and institution building, by and large, has been slow in some regions. Many Afghans are questioning where the billions of foreign aid have gone.

Afghanistan's Regional Concerns

Afghanistan's neighbors are reportedly beginning, once again, to meddle in the country's internal affairs. The Strategic Partnership that was signed between the United States and Afghanistan has created anxieties for a number of neighboring countries. Some groups in Pakistan continue to support and provide a haven for Taliban and foreign terrorists. Although the Iranian government played an important role during the year that followed the fall of the Taliban and during the Bonn Agreement process, there are reports that it is now trying to destabilize the pro-American Afghan government. Afghan officials see a direct link between Iran's shift in policy and the heightened U.S. pressure on Iran over its nuclear ambitions and Iraq. So far, Afghanistan enjoys close ties with most former Soviet Central Asian republics. However, Afghanistan's message of hope for democracy, pluralism, equal rights, and a free-market economy unnerves neighboring authoritarian and theocratic regimes. Afghan officials feel uneasy about their future in a region where their current security strategy depends on a partnership with only the United States. Afghan officials recognize that, at this point in their history, they have no other policy alternative.

What Needs to Be Done

The United States and the other NATO nations need to train and equip enough Afghan security forces to stop the Taliban insurgency, and they also need to focus aid programs on efforts that make a difference to ordinary Afghans. In addition, Afghanistan's central government needs to be empowered.

- Training and equipping the Afghan indigenous security forces so they can play a more significant role in combating the Taliban insurgency and other criminal activities should become the central focus of foreign assistance. In addition to fighting the war and keeping the peace, the training should include lessons on democracy, equality, and human rights. Afghanistan has no shortage of potential fighters. The Afghan government, with U.S. and NATO assistance, needs to make serving in its army and the police an attractive career by raising salaries and providing additional training that can be useful once soldiers and police return to civilian life. Afghan officers should be given more responsibility to lead, so that they can play leadership roles in the government and private industry once they leave the military and police.
- Empowering a professional Afghan security force should lead to further disarmament of illegal groups and create the conditions whereby opium farmers do not fear and rely on drug lords for security. Farmers would only then be encouraged to grow alternative crops.
- The NATO nations need to win the hearts and minds of the Afghans by increasing foreign aid with a multiyear development plan that features projects that improve the day-to-day lives of ordinary Afghans. That means a shift from building schools, clinics, and prisons to a focus on restoring electricity, clean water, and roads.
- Major infrastructure developments create badly needed jobs in major cities and give young Afghans reasons to build a future in Afghanistan. The benefits of these initiatives far outweigh their costs.

- Finally, Afghanistan cannot solve its problems unless it has a stronger central government. Only 20 percent of foreign aid is now managed by the Afghan government. The bulk of assistance funds is managed by international and nongovernmental organizations. Some donors have expressed reluctance to give more to the Afghan government out of the fears of mismanagement and embezzlement. But its lack of operational and budgetary control stunts the central government's institutional development and makes meeting long-term targets difficult. The Afghan government should be held accountable via a system where disbursement of funds and project performances are managed carefully, with complete transparency to donors.

Today, Afghanistan stands at a crossroads and needs the help of the international community to take the right path. Much is at stake. The NATO alliance has bet its future on success in Afghanistan, which is on the front lines in the global war on terror. The world gains from a prosperous and secure Afghanistan that does not depend on others for its security and economic health.

References

9/11 Commission Report: Final Report of the National Commission on Terrorist Attacks Upon the United States, New York: W. W. Norton, 2004.

ABC News, "Poll: Four Years After the Fall of the Taliban, Afghans Optimistic About the Future," December 7, 2005.

ABC News.BBC World Service Poll, "Afghanistan: Where Things Stand," December 2007.

Adams, John, *Risk*, London: Routledge, 1995.

"Afghanistan: Gov't Bid to Boost Police in South," *IRIN News*, March 4, 2007. As of February 19, 2008: http://www.irinnews.org/Report.aspx?ReportId=70504

Afghanistan National Development Strategy, "Benchmark Status Report March 2006 to March 2007," April 2007. As of February 19, 2008:
http://www.ands.gov.af/ands/jcmb/index.asp?j1=collapse&j2=collapse&j3=collapse&j4=collapse&j5=expand

———, "JCMB Task Force on Afghan National Police Target Strength," March 2007. As of February 19, 2008:
http://www.ands.gov.af/ands/jcmb/src/jcmb5/5B.%20Task%20Force%20on%20Police%20Ceillings.pdf

"Afghanistan Riddled with Drug Ties," *Christian Science Monitor*, May 13, 2005.

"Afghanistan: The Other War," *Time*, March 8, 2004.

"Afghanistan's Forgotten War," *New York Times*, August 6, 2005.

Altai Consulting, Afghan National Development Poll, November 2005.

Alvi, Hamid, "Troubled Pak-US Alliance," *Pakistan Times*, June 27, 2007.

Anderson, Jon W., "Khan and Khel: Dialectics of Pakhtun Tribalism," in Richard Tapper, ed., *The Conflict of Tribe and State in Iran and Afghanistan*, London, Canberra, and New York: Croom Helm and St. Martin's Press, 1983.

Associated Press, "Afghan Civilians Reportedly Killed More by U.S., NATO Than Insurgents," *U.S. Today*, June 24, 2007.

Arnold, Anthony, *The Fateful Pebble: Afghanistan's Role in the Fall of the Soviet Empire*, Novato, Calif.: Presidio Press, 1993.

Asia Foundation, *Afghanistan in 2006: A Survey of the Afghan People*, Kabul, Afghanistan, 2006.

Baev, Pavel K., "Turning Counter-Terrorism into Counter-Revolution," *European Security*, Vol. 15, No. 1, March 2006.

Balland, Daniel, "X. Political History," in Ehsan Yarshater, ed., *Encyclopædia Iranica, Vol. 1*, London: Routledge and Kegan Paul; Costa Mesa, Calif.: Mazda, 1985.

Bearak, Barry, and Taimoor Shah, "7 Children Killed in Airstrike in Afghanistan," *New York Times*, June 19, 2007.

Beck, Ulrich (Mark Ritter, trans.), *Risk Society: Towards a New Modernity*, London: Sage Publications, 1992.

Belasco, Amy, *The Cost of Iraq, Afghanistan, and Other Global War on Terror Operations Since 9/11*, CRS Report for Congress, RL33110, March 14, 2007.

Benard, Cheryl, and Olga Oliker, *Women and Human Security: The Case of Post-Conflict Afghanistan*, WIIS Words, Women in International Security, Georgetown University Press, Summer 2007.

Benard, Cheryl, Seth G. Jones, Olga Oliker, Cathryn Quantic Thurston, Brooke K. Stearns, and Kristen Cordell, *Women and Nation Building*, Santa Monica, Calif.: RAND Corporation, MG-579-CMEPP, 2008.

Bennett, Andrew, *Condemned to Repetition? The Rise, Fall, and Reprise of Soviet-Russian Military Interventionism, 1973–1996*, Cambridge, Mass.: MIT Press, 1999.

Brahimi, Lakhdar, "Shaping a Constitution: The UN's "Light Footprint" Approach in Afghanistan," United Nations Association of America, December 2004.

Caprioli, Mary, "Gender Equality and State Aggression: The Impact of Domestic Gender Equality on State First Use of Force," *International Interactions*, No. 29, 2003, pp. 195–214.

Carothers, Thomas, "Promoting Democracy and Fighting Terror," *Foreign Affairs*, January–February 2003.

Central Intelligence Agency, "Afghanistan," *The World Factbook* (accessed December 12, 2005). As of February 19, 2008:
https://www.cia.gov/library/publications/the-world-factbook/

Cohen, Ariel, ed., *Eurasia in Balance: The US and the Regional Power Shift*, Aldershot, UK: Ashgate, 2005.

Coleman, Isobel, "The Payoff from Women's Rights," *Foreign Affairs*, Vol. 83, No. 3, June 2004, pp. 80–95.

Daly, John, Kurt Meppen, Vladimir Socor, and S. Frederick Starr, *Anatomy of a Crisis: US-Uzbekistan Relations, 2001–2005*, Washington: Silk Road Paper, February 2006. As of February 20, 2008:
http://www.silkroadstudies.org/new/inside/staff_publications/books_reports.htm

Davis, Anthony, "How the Taliban Became a Military Force," in William Malley, ed., *Afghanistan and the Taliban: The Rebirth of Fundamentalism*, New York: Vanguard, 2001.

de Hoop Scheffer, Jaap, NATO Secretary General, speech at the Munich Conference of Security Policy, Munich, Germany, February 9, 2007.

Dobbins, James, *Ending Afghanistan's Civil War*, Santa Monica, Calif.: RAND Corporation, CT-271, 2007. As of February 19, 2008:
http://www.rand.org/pubs/testimonies/CT271/

———, "How to Talk to Iran," *Washington Post*, July 22, 2007, p. B7.

Dobbins, James, Seth G. Jones, Keith Crane, Andrew Rathmell, Brett Steele, Richard Teltschik, Anga R. Timilsina, *The UN's Role in Nation-Building: From the Congo to Iraq*, Santa Monica, Calif.: RAND Corporation, MG-304-RC, 2005. As of February 19, 2008:
http://www.rand.org/pubs/monographs/MG304/

Donini, Antonio, *Nation Building Unraveled: Aid Peace and Justice in Afghanistan*, Bloomfield, Conn.: Kumarian Press, Inc., 2004.

Dupree, Louis, *Afghanistan*, Princeton, N.J.: Princeton University Press, 1980.

DynCorp International, "IG Report Praises DI Police Training in Afghanistan," press release, December 4, 2006. As of February 26, 2008:
http://www.dyn-intl.com/subpage.aspx?id=219

Edburgh Consultants, "Evaluation of the Reintegration Aspects of DDR in Afghanistan's New Beginnings Programme," July 2005.

Fumento, Michael, "The Other War: Afghanistan Is Winnable, But Victory Can't Be Taken for Granted," *The Weekly Standard*, Vol. 12, No. 37, June 11, 2007. As of February 19, 2008:
http://www.weeklystandard.com/Content/Public/Articles/000/000/013/721paoob.asp

Gankovsky, Yuri, "The Durrani Empire: Taxes and Tax System, State Incomes and Expenditure," in Social Sciences Today Editorial Board, ed., *Afghanistan Past and Present*, Moscow: USSR Academy of Sciences, 1981.

German Federal Foreign Office, German Federal Ministry of the Interior, "Afghanistan for Rebuilding the Police Force in Afghanistan," May 29, 2006. As of February 26, 2008:
http://www.libertysecurity.org/article972.html

Ghubar, Mir-Muhammad Gholam, *Afghanestan dar Masir-e Tarikh* [Afghanistan in the Course of History], Mayvand, 2004.

Glantz, David M., "Introduction," in Lester W. Grau, ed., *The Bear Went Over the Mountain: Soviet Combat Tactics in Afghanistan*, London: Frank Cass, 1998.

Global Security, homepage. As of February 20, 2008:
http://www.globalsecurity.org/index.html

Goldsmid, Sir Frederic John, and Sir Oliver St. John, *Eastern Persia: An Account of the Journeys of the Persian Boundary Commission, 1870–71–72,* London: Macmillan and Co., 1876.

Grau, Lester W., *The Bear Went Over the Mountain: Soviet Combat Tactics in Afghanistan*, London: Frank Cass, 1998 (originally published in Russian in 1991).

Gregorian, Vartan, *The Emergence of Modern Afghanistan: Politics of Reform and Modernization, 1880–1946*, Stanford, Calif.: Stanford University Press, 1969.

Griswold, Eliza, "Where the Taliban Roam," *Harper's Magazine*, September 2003.

Groenewold, George, *Millennium Development Indicators of Education, Employment and Gender Equality of Afghan Refugees in Pakistan*, Office of the United Nations High Commissioner for Refugees, 2006. As of February 20, 2008:
http://www.unhcr.org/statistics/STATISTICS/45adf4122.pdf

Haqqani, Husain, *Pakistan: Between Mosque and Military,* Washington, D.C.: Carnegie Endowment for International Peace, 2005.

Harpviken, Kristian Berg, "'Afghanistan: From Buffer State to Battleground—to Bridge Between Regions?" in James Hentz and Morten Bøås, eds., *Beyond the Nation State: New and Critical Security and Regionalism*, Aldershot, UK: Ashgate, 2003.

———, "How Transnational Is the Taliban?" paper presented at the Centre for the Study of Civil War workshop, March 2007. As of February 20, 2008:
http://www.prio.no/page/CSCW_research_detail/Programme_detail_CSCW/9649/49347.html

Headquarters, Department of the Army, *Counterinsurgency*, Field Manual 3-24, Washington, D.C., June 2006.

Hobbes, Thomas, *Leviathan*, London: Everyman's Library, 1914.

Hobsbawm, Eric, *The Age of Extremes: A History of the World, 1914–1991*, New York: Vintage Books, 1994.

Hunt, Swanee, "Let Women Rule," *Foreign Affairs*, May–June 2007.

Hussain, Zahid, *Frontline Pakistan: The Struggle with Militant Islam*, New York: Columbia University Press, 2007.

Ignatieff, Michael, "Nation-Building Lite," *New York Times Magazine*, July 28, 2002, p. 26.

Inderfurth, Karl F., "Losing the 'Other War' in Afghanistan?" *International Herald Tribune*, May 29, 2007.

Inspectors General, U.S. Departments of State and Defense, *Interagency Assessment of Afghanistan Police Training and Readiness*, Report No. ISP-IQO-07-07, 2006.

International Crisis Group, *Countering Afghanistan's Insurgency: No Quick Fixes*, Report No. 123, November 2, 2006.

———, *Pakistan's Tribal Areas: Appeasing the Militants*, Crisis Group Asia Report No. 125, December 2006.

———, *Reforming Afghanistan's Police*, Crisis Group Asia Report No. 138, August 30, 2007.

International Monetary Fund, "IMF Board Approves $119.1 Million PRGF Arrangement for the Islamic Republic of Afghanistan," June 26, 2006. As of February 20, 2008:
http://www.imf.org/external/np/sec/pr/2006/pr06144.htm

International Security Assistance Force, homepage. Accessed December 12, 2005:
http://www.afnorth.nato.int/ISAF/

"Iran Envoy Lists Iranian Infrastructure Projects in Afghan Herat Province," *Islamic Republic News Agency*, October 27, 2003.

"Iran for Development, Security in Afghanistan," *IRNA*, May 28, 2007.

"Iran Rules Out US Attack," Fars News Agency (Tehran), July 30, 2007.

Isby, David C., "Afghanistan: The Soviet Victory," in Peter G. Tsouras, ed., *Cold War Hot: Alternative Decisions of the Cold War*, London: Greenhill Books, 2003.

Islamic Republic of Afghanistan, *Afghan National Development Strategy, Vol. I*, undated. As of February 26, 2008:
http://www.ands.gov.af

———, Afghanistan National Development Strategy Joint Coordination and Monitoring Board, *Annual Report*, May 2007.

———, Afghanistan National Development Strategy Joint Coordination and Monitoring Board, *JCMB Task Force on Afghan National Police Target Strength*, March 2007. As of February 26, 2008:
http://www.ands.gov.af/ands/jcmb/src/jcmb5/5B.%20Task%20Force%20on%20Police%20Ceillings.pdf

Jakobsen, Peter Viggo, *Western Use of Coercive Diplomacy After the Cold War: A Challenge for Theory and Practice*, New York: Macmillan, 1998.

———, "Har Danmark et body bag syndrom?" [Does Denmark Have a Body Bag Syndrome?], *Militært Tidsskrift*, Vol. 133, No. 1, April 2004.

———, *PRTs in Afghanistan: Successful But Not Sufficient*, Danish Institute for International Studies, DIIS Report 2005: 6. As of February 20, 2008:
http://www.diis.dk/graphics/Publications/Reports2005/pvj_prts_afghanistan.pdf

Jalali, Ali, and Lester W. Grau, "Whither the Taliban?" *The Cyber-Caravan*, March 6, 1999.

Jehl, Douglas, "A Nation Challenged: Outside Influences," *New York Times*, March 9, 2002, p. 10.

Johnson, Chris, and Jolyon Leslie, *Afghanistan: The Mirage of Peace*, New York: Zed Books, 2004.

Jones, Seth G., "Pakistan's Tribal Deals Aren't Working," *International Herald Tribune*, December 28, 2006. As of February 26, 2008:
http://www.rand.org/commentary/122806IHT.html

———, "Pakistan's Dangerous Game," *Survival*, Vol. 49, No. 1, March 2007, pp. 15–32.

Jones, Seth G., Jeremy M. Wilson, Andrew Rathmell, and K. Jack Riley, *Establishing Law and Order After Conflict*, Santa Monica, Calif.: RAND Corporation, MG-374-RC, 2005.

Kakar, M. Hasan, *Government and Society in Afghanistan—The Reign of Amir Abd Al-Rahman Khan*, Austin: University of Texas Press, 1979.

Khan, Adnan R., "The Danger Zone," *Maclean's*, November 24, 2003, p.35.

Khan, Farrukh, "Respecting Wishes of the Persian Government," Paris, December 26, 1857. FO 60/221.

Khan, Ismail, "Crackdown Launched as Tribesmen Seek Time," *Dawn*, October 10, 2003.

Khan, M. Ilyas, "Pakistan's Tribals—Who Is Killing Who?" BBC News, April 5, 2007.

Khomeini, Ayatollah Ruhollah (Hamid Algar, trans.), *Islam and Revolution*, London: Keegan Paul International, 1985.

King, Elizabeth, and Andrew Mason, *Engendering Development Through Gender Equality in Rights, Resources, and Voice,* Volume 1, A World Bank Policy Report, 2001.

Kohzad, Ali Ahmad, *Men and Events Through Eighteenth and Nineteenth Century Afghanistan*, Kabul: Historical Society of Afghanistan, no date.

Kots, Aleksandr, "Russia Returns to Afghanistan?" *Komsomolskaya Pravda*, April 20–26, 2007.

Kozlov, S., ed., *Spetsnaz GRU-2: Voina ne okonchena, istoriya prodolzhaetsya* (Spetsnaz GRU-2: The war is not over, history continues), Moscow: Russkaya Panorama, 2002.

Kramer, Mark, "Soviet Deliberations During the Polish Crisis, 1980–1981," Special Working Paper no. 1, Woodrow Wilson Center, Washington, April 1999.

Krugman, Paul, "The Math of Failure," *International Herald Tribune*, October 28–29, 2006.

Lieven, Dominic, *Empire: The Russian Empire and Its Rivals*, New Haven, Conn.: Yale University Press, 2001.

Marzban, Omid, "Mullah Dadullah: Military Mastermind of Taliban Insurgency," *Terrorism Focus*, March 21, 2006. As of February 20, 2008:
http://jamestown.org/terrorism/news/article.php?articleid=2369933

Mastny, Vojtech, "The Soviet Non-Invasion of Poland in 1980–1981 and the End of the Cold War," Woodrow Wilson Center, Cold War International History project, Working Paper no. 23, Washington, D.C., September 1998.

McMahon, Scott, "UN: 'Light Footprint' in Afghanistan Could Hold Lessons for Iraq," *Radio Liberty/Radio Free Europe*, April 2003. As of February 26, 2008:
http://www.rferl.org/features/2003/04/07042003115224.asp

Ministry of Foreign Affairs of Denmark, *Humanitarian Reconstruction Assistance to Afghanistan 2001–2005: Summary Report*, October 2005. As of February 20, 2008:
http://www.um.dk/NR/rdonlyres/F48036CB-D540-41D0-8AC3-AED57D551194/0/Afghanistan_summaryReport.pdf

Mustawfi, 'Abd Allah, *Shahr-i zindigani-i man ya tarikh-i ijtima'i va idari-i dawrah-'i qajariyah* [The Town of My Life or the History of Society and Administration of the Qajar Era], Tehran: Kitabfurushi-i Zavvar, 1964, pp. 85–86.

Nagl, John A., *Learning to Eat Soup with a Knife: Counterinsurgency Lessons from Malaya and Vietnam*, New York: Praeger, 2002.

NATO, ISAF fact sheet, no date. Accessed May 31, 2007:
http://www.nato.int/isaf/media/pdf/placemat_isaf.pdf

Newell, Richard S., "Post-Soviet Afghanistan: The Position of Minorities," *Asian Survey*, Vol. 29, No. 11, November 1989.

Niazi, Tarique, "Pakistan's Peace Deal with Taliban Militants," Jamestown Foundation, *Terrorism Monitor*, Volume 4, Issue 19, October 5, 2006.

———, "The Taliban's Turf War in South Waziristan," Jamestown Foundation, *Terrorism Focus*, Volume IV, Issue 9, April 10, 2007.

Norling, Nicklas, report on the First Kabul Conference on Partnership, Trade and Development in Greater Central Asia, Washington, April 2006. As of February 20, 2008:
http://www.silkroadstudies.org/new/docs/0604Kabul.pdf

Nourizadeh, Ali, "Iran Makes Last Minute Delegation Change Before US Meeting," *Asharq al-Awsat*, London, May 29, 2007.

O'Bryant, JoAnne, and Michael Waterhouse, *U.S. Forces in Afghanistan*, CRS Report for Congress, RS22633, March 27, 2007.

Patel, Seema, and Steven Ross, *Breaking Point: Measuring Progress in Afghanistan*, Washington, D.C.: Center for Strategic and International Studies, 2007.

Peykar, K. Pamir, *Zohour va Soghout-e A'la-Hazrat Amanullah Khan* [The Rise and Fall of His Majesty Amanullah Khan] Toronto: Pegah, 2003.

Poullada, Leon B., *Reform and Rebellion in Afghanistan, 1919–1929*, Ithaca, NY: Cornell University Press, 1973.

Quinn, Maureen, "Statement of Ambassador Maureen Quinn, Coordinator for Afghanistan, Before the U.S. House of Representatives Committee on International Relations, September 22, 2005," Washington, D.C.: U.S. Government Printing Office, 2005.

"Rafsanjani: World Should Admire Iran's Nuclear Achievements," *IRNA*, July 13, 2007.

Rahman, Abdur (Mir Munshi, ed.), *The Life of Abdur Rahman*, London: John Murray, 1990.

Rashid, Ahmed, *Taliban: The Story of the Afghan Warlords*, London: Pan Books, 2000.

———, *Taliban: Militant Islam, Oil, and Fundamentalism in Central Asia*, New Haven, Conn.: Yale University Press, 2001.

Rasmussen, Mikkel Vedby, *The Risk Society at War: Terror, Technology, and Strategy in the Twenty-First Century*, Cambridge, UK: Cambridge University Press, 2006.

Rassoul, Zalmai, National Security Advisor, Islamic State of Afghanistan, interview with the author.

Ricchiardi, Sherry, "The Forgotten War," *American Journalism Review*, August–September 2006. As of February 20, 2008:
http://www.ajr.org/Article.asp?id=4162

Robichaud, Carl, "Remember Afghanistan? A Glass Half Full, On the Titanic," *World Policy Journal*, Vol. 23, No. 1, Spring 2006, p. 21.

Rubin, Barry R., "Saving Afghanistan," *Foreign Affairs*, Vol. 86, No. 1, January–February 2007. As of February 20, 2008:
http://www.foreignaffairs.org/20070101faessay86105/barnett-r-rubin/saving-afghanistan.html

Ross, Brian, and Jill Rackmill, "Closing In: Hunt for bin Laden Narrowed to Hostile, Rugged Region of Pakistan," ABC News, September 8, 2003.

Roy, Olivier, *Islam and Resistance in Afghanistan*, Cambridge, UK: Cambridge University Press, 1986.

Rubin, Barnett R., "Lineages of the State in Afghanistan," *Asian Survey*, No. 28, 1988.

———, "The Fragmentation of Afghanistan," *Foreign Affairs*, Vol. 68, No. 5, Winter 1989/1990.

———, *Fragmentation of Afghanistan: State Formation and Collapse in the International System*, New Haven, Conn.: Yale University Press, 2000.

———, "The Political Economy of War and Peace in Afghanistan," *World Development*, Vol. 28, No. 10, 2000, pp. 1789–1803.

———, "Saving Afghanistan," *Foreign Affairs*, Vol. 86, No. 1, January–February 2006.

———, "Still Ours to Lose: Afghanistan on the Brink," prepared testimony for the House Committee on International Relations, September 20, 2006, and the Senate Committee on Foreign Relations, September 21, 2006.

———, "Still Ours to Lose: Afghanistan on the Brink," The Council on Foreign Relations, September 21, 2006. As of February 20, 2008:
http://www.cfr.org/publication/11486/still_ours_to_lose.html

Saikal, Amin, *Modern Afghanistan: A History of Struggle and Survival*, New York: I. B. Tauris, 2004.

Samii, Bill, "Mashhad Broadcasting Changes Its Tune," *Radio Free Europe/Radio Liberty (RFE/RL) Iran Report*, Vol. 5, No. 21, June 10, 2002.

———, "Herat and Iran Strengthen Ties," *Radio Free Europe/Radio Liberty (RFE/RL) Iran Report*, July 8, 2002.

Senlis Coucil, "Afghanistan Five Years Later: The Return of the Taliban," Spring/Summer 2006. As of February 20, 2008:
http://www.senliscouncil.net

Sennott, Charles M., "Afghanistan: After 5 Years, a Forgotten War?" *Boston Globe*, September 12, 2006.

Shahrani, Nazif M., "State Building and Social Fragmentation in Afghanistan—A Historical Perspective," in Ali Banuazizi and Myron Weiner, eds., *The State, Religion and Ethnic Politics: Afghanistan, Iran, and Pakistan*, New York: Syracuse University Press, 1986.

Shariatmadari, Husayn, *Ahvaz-i Kucheh-i Baghi* ("Street Garden Song"), *Kayhan* (Tehran), July 9, 2007.

Starr, S. Frederick, "A Partnership for Central Asia," *Foreign Affairs*, Vol. 84, No. 4, July–August 2005.

Stephens, Joe, and David B. Ottaway, "A Rebuilding Plan Full of Cracks," *Washington Post*, November 20, 2005.

"Taleban 'Shifting Focus to Kabul,'" BBC News, June 21, 2007. As of February 18, 2008: http://news.bbc.co.uk/go/pr/fr/-/2/hi/south_asia/6224900.stm

"Taliban Names Slain Commander's Brother as Successor," *International Herald Tribune*, May 18, 2007.

"The Taliban File," Part 111, The National Security Archive, March 19, 2004.

Tanner, Stephen, *Afghanistan: A Military History from Alexander the Great to the Fall of the Taliban*, Cambridge, Mass.: Da Capo Press, 2002.

U.S. Agency for International Development, *USAID/Afghanistan Strategic Plan, 2005–2010*, May 2005.

U.S. Department of State, *International Narcotics Control Strategy Report 2007*. As of February 20, 2008: http://www.state.gov/p/inl/rls/nrcrpt/2007/vol1/html/80858.htm

———, "Bush Announces New Plan for Afghanistan," February 15, 2007.

U.S. Government Accountability Office, *Afghanistan Reconstruction: Despite Some Progress, Deteriorating Security and Other Obstacles Continue to Threaten Achievement of U.S. Goals*, G0A-05-742, July 2005. As of February 20, 2008:
http://www.gao.gov/new.items/d05742.pdf

———, *Securing, Stabilizing, and Reconstructing Afghanistan: Key Issues for Congressional Oversight*, GAO-07-801SP, May 2007.

"US Troops Not Welcome Here, Warn Pakistani Tribal Belt Residents," Agence France Press, August 28, 2002.

United Kingdom Ministry of Defence, "Operations in Afghanistan: British Forces," Web page. As of February 20, 2008:
http://www.mod.uk/DefenceInternet/FactSheets/OperationsFactsheets/OperationsInAfghanistanBritishForces.htm

United Nations Assistance Mission in Afghanistan, "Strategy for Disbanding Illegal Armed Groups (DIAG)," November 2005.

United Nations Children's Fund, "Millions of Afghan Children Head Back to School," March 21, 2007. As of February 20, 2008:
http://www.unicef.org/media/media_39160.html

United Nations Development Programme, *Afghanistan National Human Development Report 2004: Security with a Human Face: Challenges and Responsibilities*, 2004.

———, *Afghanistan's New Beginning Programme 2005 Third Quarter Report*, AFG/03/Mo5/ND/34, undated.

United Nations High Commission for Refugees, *Statistical Summary Overview: Census of Afghans in Pakistan*, undated. As of February 20, 2008:
http://www.unhcr.org

United Nations Office on Drugs and Crime, *Afghanistan Opium Survey 2001*, 2001. As of February 20, 2008: http://www.unodc.org/pdf/publications/report_2001-10-16_1.pdf

———, *Afghanistan Opium Survey 2004*, November 2004. As of February 20, 2008: http://www.unodc.org/pdf/afg/afg_survey_2005.pdf

———, *Afghanistan Opium Survey 2005*, November 2005. As of February 20, 2008: http://www.unodc.org/pdf/afg/afg_survey_2005.pdf

———, "Afghan Opium Cultivation Soars 59 Percent in 2006, UNODC Survey Shows," press release, September 2006. As of February 20, 2008:
http://www.unodc.org/pdf/uzbekistan/Newsletter5_eng.pdf

———, *Afghanistan Opium Survey 2007*, August 2007. As of February 20, 2008: http://www.unodc.org/pdf/research/AFG07_ExSum_web.pdf

United Nations, *Secretary-General Report to the UN Security Council on the Situation in Afghanistan and Its Implications for International Peace and Security*, August 2005.

United States Department of State Inspectors, *General Interagency Assessment of Afghanistan Police Training and Readiness*, Report No. ISP-IQO-07-07, 2006.

"US: 'Irrefutable' Proof Iran Arms Taliban," CBS News. June 13, 2007. As of February 20, 2008: http://www.cbsnews.com/stories/2007/06/13/world/main2921708.shtml

van Ham, Peter, and Jorrit Kamminga, "Poppies for Peace: Reforming Afghanistan's Opium Industry," *The Washington Quarterly*, Vol. 30, No. 1, Winter 2006–2007.

Verhoturov, Dmitri, "Another Afghanistan," Expert (Web site in Russian), 2007. As of February 20, 2008: http://www.expert.ru/printissues/expert/2007/22/drugoy_afganistan/

Welch, David A., and Odd Arne Westad, *The Intervention in Afghanistan and the Fall of Détente*, Nobel Symposium 95, Oslo, 1996.

Westad, Odd Arne, *The Global Cold War*, Cambridge, UK: Cambridge University Press, 2005

White House Office of the Press Secretary, "President Outlines War Effort," April 17, 2002. As of February 20, 2008:
http://www.whitehouse.gov/news/releases/2002/04/20020417-1.html

World Bank, "Afghanistan: State Building, Sustaining Growth, and Reducing Poverty," September 9, 2004.

———, *Afghanistan: Managing Public Finances for Development, Volume IV: Improving Public Financial Management: Case Studies of Selected Sectors*, 2005.

———, "Afghanistan Country Brief," July 2005.

———, "World Development Indicators," 2005.

Zia-Zarifi, Sam, *Losing the Peace in Afghanistan*, Human Rights Watch, World Report, 2004.

Zoroya, Gregg, "Afghan Enemy Grows Fiercer," *USA Today*, November 17, 2005, p. 1A.